GW00497771

The Edible COOKIE DOUGH COOKBOOK

The Edible COOKIE DOUGH COOKBOOK

75 RECIPES FOR INCREDIBLY DELECTABLE DOUGHS
YOU CAN EAT RIGHT OFF THE SPOON

Olivia Hops

HARVARD
COMMON
PRESS

Brimming with creative inspiration, how-to projects, and useful information to enrich your everyday life, Quarto Knows is a favorite destination for those pursuing their interests and passions. Visit our site and dig deeper with our books into your area of interest: Quarto Creates, Quarto Cooks, Quarto Homes, Quarto Lives, Quarto Drives, Quarto Explores, Quarto Gifts, or Quarto Kids.

© 2018 Quarto Publishing Group USA Inc.
Text © 2018 Quarto Publishing Group USA Inc.
Photography © 2018 Leslie Grow

First Published in 2018 by
The Harvard Common Press, an imprint of The Quarto Group,
100 Cummings Center, Suite 265-D, Beverly, MA 01915, USA.
T (978) 282-9590
F (978) 283-2742
QuartoKnows.com

The Harvard Common Press titles are also available at discount for retail, wholesale, promotional, and bulk purchase. For details, contact the Special Sales Manager by email at specialsales@quarto.com or by mail at The Quarto Group, Attn: Special Sales Manager, 401 Second Avenue North, Suite 310, Minneapolis, MN 55401, USA.

22 21 20 19 18   1 2 3 4 5

ISBN: 978-1-55832-931-7

Digital edition published in 2018
eISBN: 978-1-55832-932-4

Library of Congress Cataloging-in-Publication Data is available

Design and Page Layout: www.traffic-design.co.uk
Cover Image: Glenn Scott Photography
Food Styling: Hristina Misafiris

Printed in China

Dedication

This book is dedicated to Uncle Trevor. You told me to go
for my dreams and that if I put my mind to something,
I could accomplish anything. I know it's not the book we
discussed getting published so many years ago, but I hope it
still makes you proud. I love and miss you every day.

CONTENTS

Unbaked: A Cookie Dough Journey and Primer

My road to mixing cookie dough all day long wasn't a straight one. From the time I was eleven years old, I dreamed of becoming a sports journalist. And when, only seven years later, I was sitting in my cubicle at The NFL Network editing game highlights, it seemed as if my dreams had come true faster than I had imagined they could.

I was eighteen years old and working at the company of my dreams, a company most football-loving fans would love to work at. But I wasn't cutting highlights with a smile on my face. What I thought would be an exciting job turned out to be anything but.

There were many reasons why I hated the job I had wanted so badly only a few months prior, but to put it simply, I was terribly bored. As someone who has struggled with severe anxiety my entire life, being bored made me miserable, and being miserable made me anxious. It was a suffocating cycle, and I knew I couldn't take much more of it.

One day, my boss called me into his office and proceeded to scold me, claiming my work production had fallen. Even though my anxiety was at one of its worst points in my life, I would never allow myself to slack off. Yes, I was no longer enthusiastic about coming into work, but I would have gone to battle to prove that the quality of my work had not changed. I had always been a hard worker, and if I weren't, I wouldn't have gotten the job I had at the age I was. I attempted and failed to hold back tears as I tried to tell

my boss I was simply dealing with lifelong anxiety and depression. I apologized for keeping to myself and promised I had never allowed my work to falter. When he proceeded to tell me "everyone gets sad sometimes" so "suck it up," I proceeded to quit.

I had just quit my dream job, but I wasn't upset about it. I felt a tremendous relief when I walked away from the cause of my anxiety for the last time. God was telling me it was time for a new dream.

Having moved from San Diego to Los Angeles for the job, I knew I needed to figure out another way to make money. (I would have moved home, but I had met a boy. How cliché of me!) I had decided I wanted to be my own boss in hopes that it would help with my anxiety. I had always loved baking and figured that was the way I would go. I attempted for a month to sell baked goods online before I realized my product didn't stand out in the sea of home bakers in LA. I wasn't successful at this first venture, and I started to look for a better idea.

I was anxiously watching my bank account drain too quickly when a good friend came to Los Angeles to visit me. We went to lunch by the beach and then wandered into an ice cream shop where they mixed in the toppings. As I ate my cake batter–flavored ice cream with rainbow sprinkles mixed in, an idea popped into my head. What if there were a shop where you could order cookie dough, customized like ice cream, just the way you like it. Eating cookie dough while baking had always been one of my favorite things. And if I did it, there had to be other people who loved doing it, too.

For the next month, I researched how to make cookie dough safe to eat and what my competition looked like. I tested lots of recipes. I created a name and a logo, designed a website, and signed up for social media accounts. It was April 2015 when Unbaked: A Cookie Dough Bar launched as an online shop selling customizable edible cookie dough. For months, I barely had enough money to pay rent. I only had a couple of orders a week, but I was happy, and most importantly, not anxious.

It took a while, but Unbaked went from 100 followers on Instagram and five orders a week to 40,000 followers and hundreds of orders a week. My one-woman company (run with the help of my parents, my sister, my boyfriend, and my friend Katie) was suddenly a hot trend, being featured on the Food Network's social media pages, in the *New York Times*, at the Museum of Ice Cream in Los Angeles, in *LA Weekly*, and more.

Unbaked has grown so much in the few years it's been in business that I had to hire real employees (instead of just forcing my family to help me). I now have two part-time employees helping me in the kitchen, Erin and Jonah. Erin's specialty is working the giant 20-quart (19 L) mixer (which we have named Karen). Jonah, who lives life on the autism spectrum, labels the jars of dough, tapes boxes together, and writes the notes customers request to be included in their order. They help the ship run smoothly, and without them, the business and this cookbook wouldn't be possible.

I couldn't have realized my new dream without the help of my family and friends and all of you cookie dough lovers out there. You gave me the chance to do something that makes me happy: mixing cookie dough all day.

I want to give you the chance to make that same dough in your own kitchen. In the recipes that follow, you'll learn how to make all of the flavors we offer, along with many more. My sister Natalie and the aforementioned Erin have helped me taste-test all of the recipes in these pages, and they approve!

The Edible Cookie Dough Trend

Before you start whipping up your very own delicious batches of edible cookie dough, let's first dive into the edible cookie dough trend itself. This fun and nostalgic food trend burst onto the foodie scene within the past couple of years. I mean, who didn't steal a spoonful of dough while baking with Mom or lick the beaters after Grandma blended the perfect amounts of spices for her famous oatmeal cookies? If you didn't do this (and love it) as a child, you might not be human. It's a wonder why this hasn't been a trend since the beginning of baking itself.

Besides being able to buy edible cookie dough online, cookie dough fanatics can purchase it in grocery stores, farmers' markets, and even storefronts dedicated entirely to the unique treat. If you need your fix of this addicting sweet while browsing the aisles of Bristol Farms or Gelson's Markets in Southern California, you can pick up a jar of the Cookie Dough Café's or Edoughble's dough. If you're sightseeing in New York City, you can walk into DŌ, Cookie Dough Confections' storefront, and pick yourself up an ice cream cone of dough. If your craving hits while vacationing abroad, no worries! Spooning Cookie Dough sells cups of cookie dough at their storefront in Berlin, Germany, and at street fairs across the city. In Melbourne, Australia, Cookie Dough Dream will deliver dough right to your front door—the same day if that's what you need!

For all of you who aren't close to your own edible cookie dough store or just aren't patient enough to wait for it to ship to you, this cookbook will explain how to make your very own delicious dough at home. Making dough yourself is not only a more inexpensive option, but it also allows you to personalize and customize even further. You can create your own flavor combinations, make substitutes to account for food allergies, or make your dough sweeter, saltier, thicker, thinner—anything so that it tastes perfect to your unique taste buds.

Is Cookie Dough Safe to Eat?

Now, let me address the main question you may have. Why isn't normal cookie dough safe to eat? And what makes the recipes in this book okay to eat?

Regular cookie dough isn't safe to eat for two reasons. The first reason is the raw egg it contains. Eggs can be contaminated with the bacteria *Salmonella*—the bacteria is actually on the shells, but it can contaminate the yolk and white when you crack the egg. This is only a risk when the egg is raw. When an egg is cooked, the bacteria are killed by the high temperatures. That's why eating cookie dough puts you at risk of a *Salmonella* infection but eating a baked cookie doesn't.

While *Salmonella* poisoning through eating the raw eggs in cookie dough is the most known reason as to why dough is unsafe to eat, there is also another ingredient that puts you at risk of getting sick if eaten raw. Raw flour can also cause a food-borne illness. Uncooked flour can contain the bacteria *E. coli*. This unsettling fact was discovered less than a decade ago, and few people are aware that simply omitting the eggs in cookie dough doesn't make it safe to eat. Just like with the egg, if the flour is cooked, there is no risk of getting sick, as any bacteria would be killed by the high baking temperatures.

To ensure Unbaked's Cookie Dough is edible raw and to make sure the following recipes are safe for you to indulge in, eggs are omitted and heat-treated flour is used. Heat-treated flour is flour that has been heated to at least 160°F (71°C) to ensure that any possible bacteria present in it is killed by the heat. I teach you how to heat-treat your own flour for all of your edible cookie dough on page 15. Don't worry, it's extremely easy and takes only a few minutes to do.

What Makes a Good Edible Cookie Dough?

When making your recipes, keep in mind that the best edible cookie dough recipes are ones that are mixed properly. The creaming of the butter and sugar is essential for delicious-tasting dough. Since you won't be baking the dough, you want to dissolve the sugar granules to eliminate the sandy sugar texture. Whipping the butter and sugar together for an extended period of time will help create creamy and smooth dough textures.

Whipping the butter isn't just important for making a smooth dough; it's also important in making sure your dough turns out correctly in consistency. Whipping the butter adds air to the mixture, causing it to grow in size. The flour for the recipes is then calculated to account for the extra volume of the butter. So, if you don't whip the butter, it will throw off the flour measurements and result in a dry dough.

If you choose to mix the dough by hand rather than whipping it with a mixer, it's not a death sentence for the dough. You can absolutely mix the dough by hand. But, you must make a change in the amount of flour you use, since there will be a lesser volume of butter. To do this, simply add the flour a little at a time until the dough reaches a soft and smooth texture. This will ensure that you don't accidentally add too much flour and end up with a crumbly mess.

Speaking of flour, it's essential for the flour to be measured correctly, too. Just like if the butter isn't whipped correctly, if the flour isn't measured correctly, the recipe's measurement proportions will be off. All of the flour in these recipes is fluffed before measuring. To do this, using your measuring cup, gather a cup (125 g) of flour from its container and sprinkle it back down. Do this a few times until the flour isn't packed down into its container. You can also spoon your flour into the measuring cup to achieve the same affect. The thing you absolutely don't want to do is pack the flour down into the measuring cup. This will result in you adding more flour than the recipe calls for, and thus your dough could end up very dry and crumbly.

Can I Make Substitutions?

Maybe the greatest thing about making edible cookie dough is the fact that it doesn't need to be baked. Not only does that make it an easy and quick dessert to whip up, but it also allows you to substitute ingredients on the fly. Baking is a science. If you add baking soda instead of baking powder, your baked good may be a dud. When making edible cookie dough, though, you can feel free to substitute nearly any ingredient. Since it's not ever going to be baked, changing an ingredient won't ruin the recipe like it could with regular cookie dough. So, if you want to add wheat flour instead of all-purpose, go for it. If you want to swap white sugar for brown sugar, get to swapping. If you want to make sugar-free dough, opt for a sugar substitute. If you want to make the dough vegan, just whip out the coconut oil.

How Do I Serve the Dough?

Although the traditional way of eating the dough is with a spoon, the dough is extremely versatile and can be used in countless ways. If you can think it, you can most likely create it. You can use it as frosting on a cupcake, use it as a filling in a layer cake, make truffles with it, make your own cookie dough ice cream, sandwich it between two cookies, and much more.

Dough makes a great dessert, although you can of course indulge in it at any time of the day. Some flavors, like Butter Pecan Cookie Dough (page 98), are delicious spread on a piece of toast for breakfast. The MONSTER Cookie Dough (page 60) is a great party dip and would be a perfect game-day snack.

As for how much to serve, it absolutely depends on the person. Some people can eat a lot while some people, like me, can only eat a few spoonfuls at a time. The doughs are all rich and sweet, so it just depends on how much of that richness a person can take. Each recipe in this book gives a serving guideline. Again, you could get more or fewer servings from each particular recipe depending on who is eating it. So, just keep that in mind as you whip up each batch of dough.

Can I Bake My Dough?

Baking the edible cookie doughs in this book is about the only thing you can't do with them. Because there are no eggs or other leavening ingredients (such as baking soda or baking powder), if you tried to bake the dough, it would simply melt. The main ingredient in most of these recipes is butter, and what happens to butter when it gets warm? It melts!

Baking these doughs won't result in cookies, but rather just a big liquid mess. And besides, why bake these doughs and ruin the world's greatest dessert?

How Do I Store My Dough?

Since there are no eggs in any of the doughs, most of them are actually shelf-stable, meaning they can be stored right on your kitchen counter. Yes, there is butter in the doughs, but did you know that butter is just fine stored at room temperature for up to ten days? The great debate of whether butter should be stored in the refrigerator or on the kitchen counter (which is the way I was raised) is one that may never be settled. But if you do your research, you will learn that butter is able to stay fresh at room temperature for an extended period of time. When mixed with equal amounts of sugar or salt, butter can keep even longer at room temperature. Sugar and salt can act as natural preservatives for foods because they prevent bacteria from growing.

Within this cookbook, there are some doughs that will need to be refrigerated at all times, such as Maple Bacon Cookie Dough (page 96) and Eggnog Cookie Dough (page 94), since those doughs contain other ingredients that need to be kept in the refrigerator. Other doughs can be kept for up to two weeks at room temperature, one month in the refrigerator, or up to three months in the freezer. The doughs thaw perfectly, so don't be afraid to throw them in the freezer. It won't change their taste or texture. If you do decide to store the dough in the refrigerator or freezer, it will harden. Just like butter will melt if it gets warm, it will get hard if placed in a cold environment. Allow the dough to thaw for an hour or two before eating. The dough is best eaten at room temperature so that you get the true cookie dough texture. I go into greater detail of how to store each individual dough in each recipe.

If your dough dries out while being stored, it can easily be restored to its creamy and fluffy texture by adding a bit of vegetable oil. Add 1 tablespoon (15 ml) at a time until the dough reaches your preferred texture.

I hope you are as excited to try these edible cookie dough recipes as I was to create them. Remember that you can swap the dough flavors in these recipes with other flavors you prefer. In my Peanut Butter Cookie Dough Brownie (page 106) recipe, for example, I use Peanut Butter Cookie Dough (page 71) as the swirl throughout it. If you're not a peanut butter fan, Mint Chocolate Chip Cookie Dough (page 72) would be a fantastic alternative.

Good luck, and happy un-baking!

How to Heat Treat Your Flour

Heat-treating your flour is a must to ensure your dough is safe to eat. I'll walk you through the steps of how to heat-treat your flour below. It's a simple process and takes only minutes to do. You can heat-treat your flour ahead of time, just be sure to store it in a clean container, separately from raw flour.

Materials needed:

Flour

2 microwave-safe bowls

Microwave

Spoon

Candy thermometer

Sifter

1. Measure out the amount of flour needed for the recipe you wish to make and place it in one of your microwave-safe bowls.

2. Place the bowl into the microwave and heat for 30 seconds on high. Take the bowl out of the microwave and stir the flour. It will clump together, but that's okay. Heat the flour for two additional 30-second intervals, stirring in between each interval.

3. After heating the flour for a total of 1½ minutes, place the candy thermometer into the center of the flour. The temperature should read above 160°F (71°C).

4. Place the sifter over the other bowl and sift the flour into it until no more lumps remain. Make sure the bowl is big enough that you can stir your flour in it without making a mess.

5. Allow the flour to cool completely before using it in your chosen edible cookie dough recipe.

Note:
If you don't have a thermometer, that's okay. Heating the flour for 1½ minutes is more than enough to kill any possible bacteria. If you place your finger into the center of the flour, it should be hot enough that you can't keep your finger there for more than a few seconds.

Chapter One
COOKIE DOUGHS

CHOCOLATE CHIP COOKIE DOUGH

YIELD: SERVES 6 TO 8

It doesn't get more classic than this traditional chocolate chip cookie dough. When I created this recipe, I wanted it to taste like you were licking the bowl after making a real batch of homemade chocolate chip cookies. In other words, I didn't want it to be like the artificial-tasting dough you find in ice cream. Feel free to switch the type of chocolate chips you add or even to add multiple types of chips like in Unbaked's Chocolate Chip Madness dough (we add milk, white, and dark chocolate chips).

1. In a bowl of a stand mixer fitted with the paddle attachment, cream the butter and the sugars together until light and fluffy. It should take about 30 seconds on high. Scrape down the sides of the bowl when done.

2. Add the vanilla and mix on low until combined.

3. In a medium bowl, whisk together the flour and the salt. Gradually add the flour mixture to the butter mixture, mixing on low. Mix until the flour has been fully incorporated.

4. Remove the bowl from the mixer and fold in the chocolate chips by hand.

5. Eat immediately or store in an airtight container for 2 weeks at room temperature, 1 month in the refrigerator, or 3 months in the freezer.

1 cup (225 g) unsalted butter, softened

1¼ cups (285 g) lightly packed brown sugar

¼ cup (50 g) granulated sugar

1 teaspoon vanilla extract

2 cups (250 g) heat-treated all-purpose flour (page 15)

¼ teaspoon salt

1 cup (175 g) semisweet chocolate chips

GLUTEN-FREE CHOCOLATE CHIP COOKIE DOUGH

YIELD: SERVES 6 TO 8

Here's the gluten-free version of our classic chocolate chip cookie dough recipe! The only difference is a slightly sandier texture, which comes from the gluten-free flour. Other than that, it tastes just as delicious as its gluten-containing counterpart.

1. In a bowl of a stand mixer fitted with the paddle attachment, cream the butter and the sugars together until light and fluffy. It should take about 30 seconds on high. Scrape down the sides of the bowl when done.

2. Add the vanilla and mix on low until combined.

3. In a small bowl, whisk together the flour and the salt. Gradually add the flour mixture to the butter mixture, mixing on low. Mix until the flour has been fully incorporated.

4. Remove the bowl from the mixer and fold in the chocolate chips by hand.

5. Eat immediately or store in an airtight container for 2 weeks at room temperature, 1 month in the refrigerator, or 3 months in the freezer.

1 cup (225 g) unsalted butter, softened

1¼ cups (285 g) lightly packed brown sugar

¼ cup (50 g) granulated sugar

1 teaspoon vanilla extract

1¾ cups (220 g) heat-treated gluten-free flour (page 15)

¼ teaspoon salt

1 cup (175 g) semisweet chocolate chips

MATCHA GREEN TEA COOKIE DOUGH

YIELD: SERVES 6 TO 8

With matcha being all the craze lately, I knew I had to incorporate it into a dough. When working with the Japanese green tea powder, I found that the flavor grew stronger as it sat. So, if you're making the dough ahead of time, keep in mind that the matcha taste will get stronger the longer it sits before you eat it.

1. In the bowl of a stand mixer fitted with the paddle attachment, cream the butter and sugar together until light and fluffy. It should take about 30 seconds on high. Scrape down the sides of the bowl when done.

2. In a medium bowl, whisk together the flour, matcha powder, and salt. Gradually add the flour mixture to the butter mixture. Mix on low until fully incorporated.

3. Eat immediately or store in an airtight container for 2 weeks at room temperature, 1 month in the refrigerator, or 3 months in the freezer.

1 cup (225 g) unsalted butter, softened

1 cup (200 g) sugar

2 cups (250 g) heat-treated all-purpose flour (page 15)

1 tablespoon (6 g) matcha green tea powder

¼ teaspoon salt

BIRTHDAY CAKE COOKIE DOUGH

YIELD: SERVES 6 TO 8

This is the flavor that inspired it all! As I ate my cake batter-flavored ice cream when I first had the idea for Unbaked, I knew I wanted birthday cake to be a main flavor. I set out to create a recipe that tastes just like that ice cream and just like the real stuff. I truly think I accomplished that. This is the perfect flavor to serve at birthday parties, and it can be easily doubled for large parties. You can also swap out the all-purpose flour for gluten-free flour and the regular cake mix for a gluten-free version.

1. In a bowl of a stand mixer fitted with the paddle attachment, cream the butter and sugar together until light and fluffy. It should take about 30 seconds on high. Scrape down the sides of the bowl when done.

2. Add the vanilla and mix on low until combined.

3. In a medium bowl, whisk together the flour, cake mix, and salt. Gradually add the flour mixture to the butter mixture, mixing on low. Mix until the flour has been fully incorporated.

4. Remove the bowl from the mixer and fold in the rainbow sprinkles by hand.

5. Eat immediately or store in an airtight container for 2 weeks at room temperature, 1 month in the refrigerator, or 3 months in the freezer.

1 cup (225 g) unsalted butter, softened

1 cup (200 g) sugar

½ teaspoon vanilla extract

1 cup (125 g) heat-treated all-purpose flour (page 15)

1 cup (125 g) boxed yellow cake mix

¼ teaspoon salt

½ cup (60 g) rainbow sprinkles

Note:
Birthday Cake is by far Unbaked's most popular flavor. It's YouTube star Teala Dunn's favorite flavor, too. She orders several times a month!

WHITE CHOCOLATE CHAI COOKIE DOUGH

YIELD: SERVES 6 TO 8

I'm not a tea fan, but boy did I love this chai dough! It actually turned out to be one of my favorite flavors. I wasn't even sure what chai tasted like when my sister first brought it to my attention. To my surprise, it had beautiful sweet ginger undertones. To me, it's very reminiscent of a spice cake or a gingerbread cookie. This recipe is perfect for the holidays or just on a chilly night.

1. To make the white chocolate swirl, place the white chocolate chips and cream in a small microwave-safe bowl. Microwave on high for 30 seconds and then mix until a thick, smooth ganache forms. If some of the white chocolate chips remain unmelted, heat in 15-second intervals until all of the white chocolate has melted.

2. Allow the ganache to cool completely in the refrigerator, stirring occasionally to prevent a film from forming on the top. It should be cooled in about 30 minutes.

3. While it cools, to make the dough, cream the butter and sugar together in the bowl of a stand mixer fitted with the paddle attachment until light and fluffy. It should take about 30 seconds on high. Scrape down the sides of the bowl when done.

4. In a small bowl, whisk together the flour, chai powder, and salt. Gradually add the flour mixture to the butter mixture. Mix on low until fully incorporated.

5. When the ganache is cool, scoop it into the dough. Gently swirl it throughout the dough using a spoon, making sure not to completely incorporate it.

6. Eat immediately or store in an airtight container for 1 month in the refrigerator or 3 months in the freezer.

For white chocolate ganache:

½ cup (112 g) white chocolate chips

1 tablespoon (15 ml) heavy cream

For cookie dough:

1 cup (225 g) unsalted butter, softened

1 cup (200 g) sugar

1¼ cups (157 g) heat-treated all-purpose flour (page 15)

2 tablespoons (12 g) chai tea latte powder

¼ teaspoon salt

APPLE PIE COOKIE DOUGH

YIELD: SERVES 6 TO 8

You can forget about serving actual apple pie next Thanksgiving, because this apple pie cookie dough will blow your family's socks off! The homemade chunky applesauce tastes just like the sweet filling of a real apple pie. It's full of cinnamon and nutmeg flavor, and the piecrust adds a crunchy texture you'd get in the real thing.

1. Preheat the oven to 375°F (190°C, or gas mark 5). Line a baking sheet with parchment paper.

2. To make the crust, place the half round of dough on the lined baking sheet. Sprinkle the sugar evenly over the top. With a rolling pin, gently roll over the sugared dough to press the sugar into the dough.

3. Bake the crust for 22 to 25 minutes until golden brown and cooked through. Let it cool and reserve.

4. To make the applesauce, cut the apple into small chunks. Place the apple, sugars, cinnamon, nutmeg, salt, and water in a medium saucepan. Stir the ingredients together and then cover. Simmer on medium heat until the water has nearly all evaporated and the apples are soft. If the water evaporates and the apples are still too firm, just add another ¼ cup (60 ml) of water and continue to simmer until the apples are completely soft.

5. When the apples are cooked, mash them into a chunky applesauce. I use a fork, but feel free to use a potato masher or another instrument of your choice. Place it in the refrigerator and allow to cool completely, about 30 minutes.

For piecrust:

½ of a round of refrigerated pie dough, thawed to room temperature

1 tablespoon (13 g) granulated sugar

For applesauce:

1 medium apple (I used a Granny Smith, but you can use any kind).

1 tablespoon (15 g) brown sugar

1 teaspoon granulated sugar

¼ teaspoon ground cinnamon

⅛ teaspoon ground nutmeg

⅛ teaspoon salt

½ cup (120 ml) water

6. While the applesauce cools, to make the cookie dough, cream the butter and the sugars together in the bowl of a stand mixer fitted with the paddle attachment until light and fluffy. It should take about 30 seconds on high. Scrape down the sides of the bowl when done.

7. Add the vanilla and mix until combined.

8. In a medium bowl, whisk together the flour, cinnamon, nutmeg, and salt. Gradually add the flour mixture to the butter mixture. Mix on low until the flour is fully incorporated.

9. Carefully break up the piecrust into bite-size pieces. Fold in the pieces by hand until combined. Add the cooled applesauce and swirl it in.

10. Eat immediately or store in an airtight container for 1 month in the refrigerator or 3 months in the freezer.

For cookie dough:

1 cup (225 g) unsalted butter, softened

¾ cup (170 g) lightly packed brown sugar

¼ cup (50 g) granulated sugar

½ teaspoon vanilla extract

2 cups (250 g) heat-treated all-purpose flour

½ teaspoon ground cinnamon

¼ teaspoon ground nutmeg

⅛ teaspoon salt

PUMPKIN PIE COOKIE DOUGH

YIELD: SERVES 6 TO 8

Pumpkin pie is one of my favorite desserts, and this dough tastes just like pie in dough form. I incorporated the taste of pumpkin and pumpkin spice in several ways to ensure that the pumpkin flavor is the star. The addition of pumpkin purée really makes the dough taste like pumpkin pie rather than just pumpkin spice. The piecrust is an extra step you won't want to skip. It gives the dough a great crunch and diversifies the texture.

1. Preheat the oven to 375°F (190°C, or gas mark 5). Line a baking sheet with parchment paper.

2. To make the crust, place the half round of dough on the lined baking sheet. Sprinkle the sugar evenly over the top. With a rolling pin, gently roll over the sugared dough to press the sugar into the dough.

3. Bake the crust for 22 to 25 minutes until golden brown and cooked through. Let it cool and reserve.

4. To make the cookie dough, cream the butter and the sugars together in the bowl of a stand mixer fitted with the paddle attachment until light and fluffy. It should take about 30 seconds on high. Scrape down the sides of the bowl when done.

5. Add the vanilla and mix until combined. Add the pumpkin purée and mix until combined.

6. In a medium bowl, whisk together the flour, pumpkin cake mix, pumpkin pie spice, and salt. Gradually add the flour mixture to the butter mixture. Mix on low until fully incorporated.

7. Carefully break up the piecrust into bite-size pieces. Fold it into the dough by hand.

8. Eat immediately or store in an airtight container for 1 month in the refrigerator or 3 months in the freezer.

For piecrust:

½ of a round of refrigerated pie dough, thawed to room temperature

1 tablespoon (13 g) granulated sugar

For cookie dough:

1 cup (225 g) unsalted butter, softened

½ cup (115 g) lightly packed brown sugar

¼ cup plus 2 tablespoons (6 g) granulated sugar

¼ teaspoon vanilla extract

2 tablespoons (31 g) pumpkin purée

1½ cups (188 g) heat-treated all-purpose flour (page 15)

1 cup (125 g) pumpkin cake mix

½ teaspoon pumpkin pie spice

½ teaspoon salt

CANDY CANE COOKIE DOUGH

YIELD: SERVES 6 TO 8

Peppermint fans, this is the dough for you. This is another one of my all-time favorite flavors. The dough has a subtle peppermint flavor, while the candy cane bark adds the main kick of peppermint and crunch that really makes this dough extraordinary. Keep in mind that it's easy to make peppermint too strong, so be careful when measuring out the extract.

1. To make the bark, place the candy canes in a resealable plastic bag. Using a rolling pin or another heavy kitchen utensil, break the candy canes into small pieces. They should become almost a dust with some small chunks of candy canes still present.

2. In a small microwave-safe bowl, heat the chocolate chips, stirring after 20-second intervals, until the chips are completely melted.

3. Pour the melted chocolate onto a baking sheet lined with parchment paper. Use an offset spatula to spread the chocolate to about ⅛ inch (3 mm) thick.

4. Sprinkle the candy cane dust evenly onto the chocolate. Place the bark in the refrigerator and allow to firm up, about 20 minutes.

5. While the bark hardens, to make the cookie dough, cream the butter and sugar together in the bowl of a stand mixer fitted with the paddle attachment until light and fluffy. It should take about 30 seconds on high. Scrape down the sides of the bowl when done.

6. Add the peppermint extract and mix until combined.

7. In a small bowl, whisk together the flour and salt. Gradually add the flour mixture to the butter mixture. Mix on low until fully incorporated.

8. Mix in the food coloring, if using, until the dough turns a light pink color. If you prefer a deeper pink, just add more coloring until you reach your desired color.

9. Carefully break the bark up into bite-size chunks. Fold it into the dough by hand.

10. Eat immediately or store in an airtight container for 2 weeks at room temperature, 1 month in the refrigerator, or 3 months in the freezer.

For white chocolate candy cane bark:

2 standard-size candy canes

½ cup (112 g) white chocolate chips

For cookie dough:

1 cup (225 g) unsalted butter, softened

1 cup (200 g) sugar

½ teaspoon peppermint extract

1½ cups (188 g) heat-treated all-purpose flour (page 15)

¼ teaspoon salt

3 to 5 drops pink or red food coloring (optional)

GINGERBREAD COOKIE DOUGH

YIELD: SERVES 6 TO 8

Gingerbread is a holiday favorite, and this gingerbread dough is spicy with an intense kick of ginger. I use a gingerbread cake mix to give this recipe a wonderful flavor. I attempted to do a traditional recipe that included molasses, but after a few attempts where the molasses flavor was just too overwhelming, I realized I had to switch gears. Don't worry, though: You won't miss the molasses. This dough is everything you want in a gingerbread dessert.

1. In the bowl of a stand mixer fitted with the paddle attachment, cream the butter and the sugars together until light and fluffy. It should take about 30 seconds on high. Scrape down the sides of the bowl when done.

2. Add the vanilla and mix until combined.

3. In a medium bowl, whisk together the flour, gingerbread mix, ginger, and salt. Gradually add the flour mixture to the butter mixture. Mix on low until the flour is fully incorporated.

4. Eat immediately or store in an airtight container for 2 weeks at room temperature, 1 month in the refrigerator, or 3 months in the freezer.

1 cup (225 g) unsalted butter, softened

½ cup (115 g) lightly packed brown sugar

½ cup (100 g) granulated sugar

¼ teaspoon vanilla extract

1¼ cups (157 g) heat-treated all-purpose flour (page 15)

1 cup (125 g) gingerbread cake/cookie mix

½ teaspoon ground ginger

⅛ teaspoon salt

LEMON BAR COOKIE DOUGH

YIELD: SERVES 6 TO 8

This is a special recipe to me because it reminds me of baking with my mom—we used to always make lemon bars on Easter. While this recipe is more complicated and takes a little longer to make, it is absolutely worth it. It has a wonderful tart lemon flavor, and with the addition of real shortbread, it tastes like a true lemon bar. If you don't have time to make the whole recipe or only want a simple lemon-flavored dough, just follow the instructions for the cookie dough and add an additional two teaspoons of lemon zest. Feel free to swap out the lemon for another citrus flavor such as orange or lime.

1. Preheat the oven to 350°F (180°C, or gas mark 4). Line a baking sheet with parchment paper.

2. To make the crust, cream together the butter and confectioners' sugar in a medium bowl. Add the vanilla and mix until combined.

3. Add the flour and salt and mix. The dough will be very crumbly. That's okay. Dump the dough onto a cutting board and knead until the dough comes together into a ball.

4. Place the ball of dough onto the lined baking sheet and using a rolling pin, roll to a ¼-inch (6 mm) thickness. The dough may crack while you're rolling it out, but that's okay. It doesn't need to look pretty because it will be broken up later.

5. Bake the dough for 17 to 19 minutes until the edges are golden brown. Set aside and allow it to cool.

6. To make the lemon curd, cream the butter and sugar together in a medium bowl. Add the egg and whisk until smooth. Whisk the lemon zest, lemon juice, and salt into the butter mixture and mix until combined.

7. Transfer the mixture to a small pot and heat on medium-low heat for about 2 minutes, whisking often, until the mixture just begins to simmer. It should have begun to thicken at this point. Immediately remove from the heat and allow it to cool completely. Stir occasionally to keep a film from settling over the top of the

For shortbread crust:

2 tablespoons (28 g) unsalted butter, softened

¼ cup (30 g) confectioners' sugar

⅛ teaspoon vanilla extract

¾ cup plus 2 tablespoons (110 g) heat-treated all-purpose flour (page 15)

Pinch of salt

For lemon curd:

2 tablespoons (28 g) unsalted butter, softened

½ cup (100 g) granulated sugar

1 egg

2 teaspoons packed lemon zest

¼ cup (60 ml) lemon juice

Pinch of salt

For cookie dough:

1 cup (225 g) unsalted butter, softened

1 cup (200 g) granulated sugar

2 teaspoons packed lemon zest

1 tablespoon (15 ml) lemon juice

1¾ cups (220 g) heat-treated all-purpose flour (page 15)

¼ teaspoon salt

curd. Keep in mind that the curd will thicken as it cools, so don't worry if it seems too runny while hot.

8. To make the cookie dough, cream the butter and sugar together in the bowl of a stand mixer fitted with the paddle attachment until light and fluffy. It should take about 30 seconds on high. Scrape down the sides of the bowl when done.

9. Add the lemon zest and lemon juice and mix until combined.

10. In a small bowl, whisk together the flour and salt. Gradually add the flour mixture to the butter mixture. Mix on low until fully incorporated.

11. When the shortbread round has cooled, break it up into bite-size pieces. Add the pieces to the dough and fold them in by hand.

12. When the lemon curd has cooled completely, add it to the dough. Swirl it throughout the dough using a spoon, but do not fully combine.

13. Eat immediately or store in an airtight container for 1 month in the refrigerator or 3 months in the freezer.

LEMON CARDAMOM COOKIE DOUGH

YIELD: SERVES 6 TO 8

I was trying to think of a dough flavor that incorporated a "fancy" spice into it. I was watching a cooking show, and they created a dish that included lemon and cardamom. I had no idea what cardamom tasted like, but I wanted to find out. When I bought some, I was pleasantly surprised by its lemony, gingery tones. This dough has a wonderful bright flavor that reminds me of summer. The lemon flavor pops in your mouth, and the cardamom is gentle on the back end.

1. Place the sugar in a small bowl and add the zest. Using a metal spoon, grind the zest into the sugar. You want to really bring out the lemon flavor and create a lemon sugar. You will know the sugar is ready when it's a pale yellow color and slightly clumpy.

2. In the bowl of a stand mixer fitted with the paddle attachment, cream the butter and lemon sugar together until light and fluffy. It should take about 30 seconds on high. Scrape down the sides of the bowl when done.

3. In a small bowl, whisk together the flour, cardamom, and salt. Gradually add the flour mixture to the butter mixture. Mix on low until the flour is fully incorporated.

4. Eat immediately or store in an airtight container for 2 weeks at room temperature, 1 month in the refrigerator, or 3 months in the freezer.

1 cup (100 g) sugar

Zest of 2 small lemons

1 cup (225 g) unsalted butter, softened

1½ cups (188 g) heat-treated all-purpose flour (page 15)

2 teaspoons ground cardamom

¼ teaspoon salt

KEY LIME PIE COOKIE DOUGH

YIELD: SERVES 6 TO 8

This recipe is a take on the classic key lime pie. It's a simple dough that packs a giant punch of lime flavor. If you don't have key limes, that's totally fine. Just use whatever limes are available to you.

1. Place the sugar in a small bowl and add the zest. Using a metal spoon, grind the zest into the sugar. You want to really bring out the lime flavor and create a lime sugar. You will know the sugar is ready when it's a pale green color and slightly clumpy.

2. In the bowl of a stand mixer fitted with the paddle attachment, cream the butter and lime sugar together until light and fluffy. It should take about 30 seconds on high. Scrape down the sides of the bowl when done.

3. Add the lime juice and mix until combined.

4. In a medium bowl, whisk together the flour and salt. Gradually add the flour mixture to the butter mixture. Mix on low until the flour is fully incorporated.

5. Fold in the graham cracker crumbs by hand.

6. Eat immediately or store in an airtight container for 2 weeks at room temperature, 1 month in the refrigerator, or 3 months in the freezer.

1 cup (200 g) sugar

Zest of 2 key limes

1 cup (225 g) unsalted butter, softened

2 tablespoons (28 g) key lime juice (about the juice of 1 lime)

2 cups (250 g) heat-treated all-purpose flour (page 15)

⅛ teaspoon salt

¼ cup (21 g) graham cracker crumbs (about 2 full-size graham crackers)

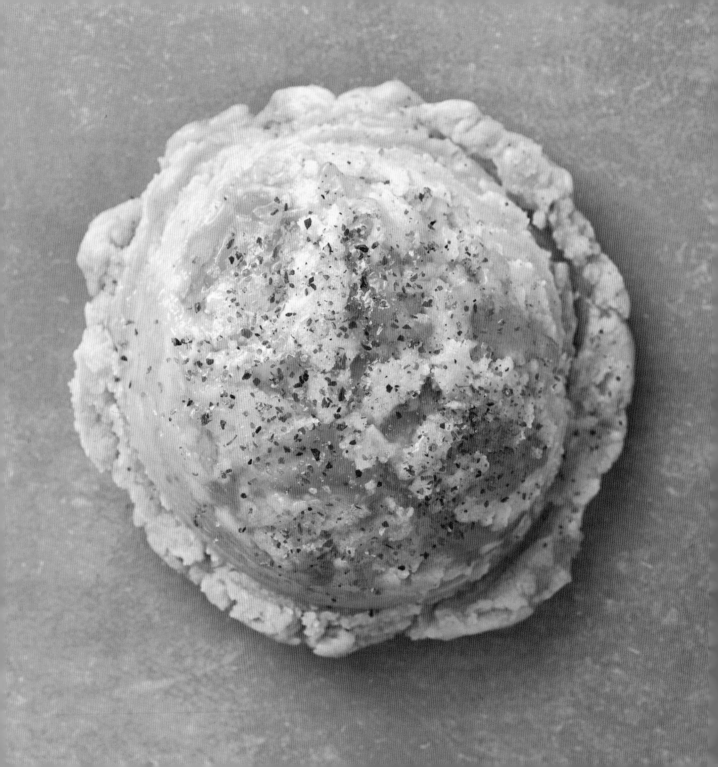

MANGO TAJÍN COOKIE DOUGH

YIELD: SERVES 6 TO 8

I created this recipe in honor of my boyfriend, Alex. We are annual pass holders at Disneyland, and every time we go, he has to get his cup of mango with Tajín at one of the fruit snack stands. Tajín is a Mexican condiment of chiles, lime, and salt. I personally cannot handle spicy foods (I can't help it—I'm a big baby!), but if you can, feel free to add all of the Tajín your heart desires.

1. In the bowl of a stand mixer fitted with the paddle attachment, cream the butter and sugar together until light and fluffy. It should take about 30 seconds on high. Scrape down the sides of the bowl when done.

2. In a small bowl, whisk together the flour, gelatin powder, and salt. Gradually add the flour mixture to the butter mixture. Mix on low until fully incorporated.

3. In a small bowl, mix the jam and Tajín until combined. Add the jam mixture to the dough and swirl it throughout using a spoon, making sure not to completely incorporate it.

4. Sprinkle more Tajín on top, depending on how much heat you want in the dough.

5. Eat immediately or store in an airtight container for 2 weeks at room temperature, 1 month in the refrigerator, or 3 months in the freezer.

1 cup (225 g) unsalted butter, softened

1 cup (200 g) sugar

1¾ cups (220 g) heat-treated all-purpose flour (page 15)

¼ cup (28 g) mango-flavored gelatin powder (I use Jell-O brand Simply Good mango passion fruit flavor.)

¼ teaspoon salt

½ cup (160 g) mango jam

2 teaspoons Tajín plus more for topping

CHOCOLATE COOKIE DOUGH

YIELD: SERVES 6 TO 8

This recipe has a rich and decadent chocolate flavor and is a perfect treat for all of the chocolate fanatics out there. The texture of this dough is extra soft and creamy from the chocolate syrup, almost like a chocolate mousse. If you are a mint fan, add half a teaspoon of peppermint extract for a truly amazing minty chocolate experience. This dough would be great as frosting on a vanilla cupcake, too.

1. In the bowl of a stand mixer fitted with the paddle attachment, cream the butter and the sugars together until light and fluffy. It should take about 30 seconds on high. Scrape down the sides of the bowl when done.

2. Add the chocolate syrup and mix until combined.

3. In a small bowl, whisk together the flour, cocoa powder, and salt. Gradually add the flour mixture to the butter mixture. Mix on low until the flour is fully incorporated.

4. Eat immediately or store in an airtight container for 2 weeks at room temperature, 1 month in the refrigerator, or 3 months in the freezer.

1 cup (225 g) unsalted butter, softened

½ cup (100 g) granulated sugar

¼ cup (60 g) lightly packed brown sugar

⅓ cup (80 ml) chocolate syrup

1¼ cups (157 g) heat-treated all-purpose flour (page 15)

3 tablespoons (15 g) unsweetened cocoa powder

⅛ teaspoon salt

Notes:
Here are a few flavor combinations you can make with this dough!
Rocky Road: Add ½ cup (25 g) mini marshmallows and ¼ cup (about 28 g) nuts of choice (such as pecans or walnuts).
Chocolate Peanut Butter Dream: Add ½ cup (94 g) Reese's Pieces and ½ cup (120 g) peanut butter chips.
S'mores Lovin': Add ½ cup (25 g) mini marshmallows and ¼ cup (21 g) graham cracker crumbs.

WHITE CHOCOLATE COOKIE DOUGH

YIELD: SERVES 6 TO 8

White chocolate can be a delicate flavor to work with, but this recipe really makes it the focal point of the dough. White chocolate ganache is added directly to the dough to give it a creamy and rich white chocolate flavor and silky texture. This recipe will work with butterscotch chips in place of white chocolate chips, too, so if you're a butterscotch fan, definitely give that a try.

1. In a small microwave-safe bowl, combine the white chocolate chips and cream. Heat for 30 seconds on high and then mix until a smooth, thick ganache forms. If the white chocolate chips haven't all melted, heat in 15-second intervals until all of the chips have melted.

2. Place the ganache in the fridge until completely cooled, about 20 minutes. The ganache doesn't need to be cold, but make sure it's not warm or it will melt the butter.

3. While the ganache chills, in the bowl of a stand mixer fitted with the paddle attachment, cream the butter and sugar together until light and fluffy. It should take about 30 seconds on high. Scrape down the sides of the bowl when done.

4. Add the cooled ganache and mix until combined.

5. In a small bowl, whisk together the flour and salt. Gradually add the flour mixture to the butter mixture. Mix on low until the flour is fully incorporated.

6. Eat immediately or store in an airtight container for 1 month in the refrigerator or 3 months in the freezer.

¾ cup (168 g) white chocolate chips

2 tablespoons (28 ml) heavy cream

1 cup (225 g) unsalted butter, softened

¾ cup (150 g) sugar

2¼ cups (281 g) heat-treated all-purpose flour (page 15)

⅛ teaspoon salt

VEGAN PIÑA COLADA COOKIE DOUGH

YIELD: SERVES 6 TO 8

When people hear there are no eggs in Unbaked's dough, they always ask if it's vegan. Unfortunately, it's not, due to the butter we use. This recipe is for all of the vegan cookie dough lovers out there who have patiently waited for me to create a vegan flavor. I decided to play off of the use of coconut oil and use it to my advantage to create this extremely flavorful dough. If you aren't vegan, don't be scared to try this recipe. You can't tell it's not made with butter!

1. In the bowl of a stand mixer fitted with the paddle attachment, mix together the coconut oils until completely combined.

2. Add the sugar to the coconut oil mixture and cream together for 30 seconds on high. Scrape down the sides of the bowl when done.

3. In a medium bowl, combine the flour and salt and whisk until combined. Gradually add the flour mixture to the coconut oil mixture and mix until fully incorporated.

4. Add the pineapple preserves and mix until the preserves are evenly mixed throughout the dough.

5. Eat immediately or store in an airtight container for 1 month in the refrigerator or 3 months in the freezer.

1 cup (225 g) unflavored coconut oil (Look for a brand with no coconut flavor or aroma.)

2 tablespoons (28 g) coconut oil (Look for a brand with a strong flavor and aroma.)

1 cup (200 g) sugar

2 cups (250 g) heat-treated all-purpose flour (page 15)

¼ teaspoon salt

¼ cup plus 2 tablespoons (120 g) pineapple preserves

COCONUT COOKIE DOUGH

YIELD: SERVES 6 TO 8

My favorite frozen yogurt flavor is coconut, and this recipe is very reminiscent of that. It's creamy and has a fantastic coconut flavor from the coconut oil. Make sure you use a coconut oil that has good coconut flavor, like a virgin coconut oil, or you won't get the correct taste. If you'd like to make this dough vegan, swap the butter for a coconut oil that doesn't have coconut flavor, like a refined coconut oil. This will keep the coconut flavor from being overwhelming.

1. In a blender or food processor, blend the coconut flakes until they become finer flakes. It should take about 30 seconds. Set aside.

2. In the bowl of a stand mixer fitted with the paddle attachment, cream the butter, coconut oil, and sugar together until light and fluffy. It should take about 30 seconds on high. Scrape down the sides of the bowl when done.

3. In a small bowl, whisk together the flour, salt, and the reserved coconut flakes. Gradually add the flour mixture to the butter mixture. Mix on low until fully incorporated.

4. Eat immediately or store in an airtight container for 2 weeks at room temperature, 1 month in the refrigerator, or 3 months in the freezer.

½ cup (43 g) sweetened coconut flakes

1 cup (225 g) unsalted butter, softened

2 tablespoons (28 g) coconut oil

1 cup (200 g) sugar

1½ cups (188 g) heat-treated all-purpose flour (page 15)

¼ teaspoon salt

RED VELVET COOKIE DOUGH

YIELD: SERVES 6 TO 8

My favorite cupcake flavor from a famous cupcake bakery near my house is their red velvet cupcake with cream cheese frosting. Red velvet is a trendy flavor, and this dough will meet all of your red velvet needs. It's a very popular flavor on UnbakedBar.com, and nearly everyone pairs it with white chocolate chips as their topping. It resembles the classic cream cheese frosting pairing, so definitely give it a shot!

1. In the bowl of a stand mixer fitted with the paddle attachment, cream the butter and the sugars together until light and fluffy. It should take about 30 seconds on high. Scrape down the sides of the bowl when done.

2. Add the chocolate syrup and mix until combined.

3. In a small bowl, whisk together the flour, cocoa powder, and salt. Add the flour mixture to the butter mixture. Mix on low until the flour is fully incorporated.

4. Begin to add the red food coloring and mix until all of the dough turns a bright red. If the dough isn't red enough for you, just keep adding until it reaches your desired red color.

5. Eat immediately or store in an airtight container for 2 weeks at room temperature, 1 month in the refrigerator, or 3 months in the freezer.

1 cup (225 g) unsalted butter, softened

½ cup (115 g) lightly packed brown sugar

½ cup (100 g) granulated sugar

1 tablespoon (15 ml) chocolate syrup

1¾ cups (220 g) heat-treated all-purpose flour (page 15)

1 tablespoon (5 g) unsweetened cocoa powder

⅛ teaspoon salt

1 to 2 teaspoons red food coloring

Note:

When adding the red food coloring, add a little bit at a time. Food colorings vary vastly with how potent they are. Some red colorings may only turn the dough pink, while others may only take a few drops to make the dough a bright red. Also keep in mind that food coloring strengthens over time, so if you're making the dough ahead of time, it will most likely be more red the next day!

OREO COOKIE DOUGH

YIELD: SERVES 6 TO 8

This isn't a cookies 'n' cream dough—this is a straight-up Oreo dough. You are basically eating an Oreo in dough form. How cool is that? This recipe was inspired by Alex's favorite ice cream flavor at a unique ice cream shop by our house. I'd never seen an all-Oreo ice cream before, but when I did, I knew I had to make a dough version. Add extra Oreo pieces for even more Oreo flavor.

1. In a food processor or blender, grind the Oreos to very fine crumbs. Make them as fine as you can get them. Set aside.

2. In the bowl of a stand mixer fitted with the paddle attachment, cream the butter and sugar together until light and fluffy. It should take about 30 seconds on high. Scrape down the sides of the bowl when done.

3. Add the Oreo crumbs and whip on high for another 30 seconds or so.

4. In a small bowl, whisk together the flour and salt. Gradually add the flour mixture to the butter mixture. Mix on low until the flour is fully incorporated.

5. Eat immediately or store in an airtight container for 2 weeks at room temperature, 1 month in the refrigerator, or 3 months in the freezer.

1½ cups (120 g) fine Oreo crumbs (about 18 whole Oreos)

1 cup (225 g) unsalted butter, softened

¾ cup (150 g) sugar

1½ cups (188 g) heat-treated all-purpose flour (page 15)

⅛ teaspoon salt

BROWNIE BATTER COOKIE DOUGH

YIELD: SERVES 8 TO 10

I didn't just sneak spoonfuls of cookie dough as a kid. I snuck spoonfuls of brownie batter, too. I didn't discriminate against any unbaked goods! This dough has a fudgy brownie taste that won't make you miss eating the real thing. Add some walnuts or chocolate chunks for crunch and extra flavor in your dough.

1. In a small bowl, measure out ¼ cup (32 g) of the brownie mix. Add the water and mix until a thick batter forms. It will be almost like a paste, and that's exactly what you want.

2. Place the brownie paste and butter in the bowl of a stand mixer fitted with the paddle attachment. Mix on low until fully incorporated.

3. Add the sugar and cream the butter mixture and sugar together until light and fluffy. It should take about 30 seconds on high. Scrape down the sides of the bowl when done.

4. Add the chocolate syrup and vanilla and mix until combined.

5. In a medium bowl, whisk together the flour, cocoa powder, salt, and remaining 1 cup (125 g) of brownie mix. Gradually add the flour mixture to the butter mixture. Mix on low until the flour is fully incorporated.

6. Eat immediately or store in an airtight container for 2 weeks at room temperature, 1 month in the refrigerator, or 3 months in the freezer.

1¼ cups (157 g) brownie mix

2 teaspoons water

1 cup (225 g) unsalted butter, softened

¾ cup (150 g) sugar

⅓ cup (80 ml) chocolate syrup

¼ teaspoon vanilla extract

1¾ cups (220 g) heat-treated all-purpose flour (page 15)

1 tablespoon (5 g) unsweetened cocoa powder

⅛ teaspoon salt

NUTELLA COOKIE DOUGH

YIELD: SERVES 6 TO 8

I always like to joke that I knew about Nutella before any of my friends. Nutella was a little-known food in the United States until fairly recently. I discovered it in Italy, back when I was about four years old. My dad's business is partly located there, and I was blessed to be able to live there in the summer in our apartment, which we still have today. Peanut butter wasn't the easiest to find there, so Nutella was the go-to snack! This dough is packed with Nutella flavor and is perfect for the die-hard fans out there.

1. In the bowl of a stand mixer fitted with the paddle attachment, cream the butter, sugar, and Nutella together for about 30 seconds on high. Scrape down the sides of the bowl when done.

2. Add the vanilla and mix until combined.

3. In a small bowl, whisk together the flour and salt. Gradually add the flour mixture to the butter mixture. Mix on low until the flour is fully incorporated.

4. Eat immediately or store in an airtight container for 2 weeks at room temperature, 1 month in the refrigerator, or 3 months in the freezer.

¾ cup (167 g) unsalted butter, softened

¾ cup (150 g) sugar

½ cup (148 g) Nutella

¼ teaspoon vanilla extract

1¼ cups (156 g) heat-treated all-purpose flour (page 15)

⅛ teaspoon salt

Note:
Make sure to add the flour slowly to this dough. This dough can dry out very quickly, so proceed carefully, just in case the flour is packed in or the butter isn't whipped enough (or even if the weather is off). If the dough does accidentally dry out, add a tablespoon (15 ml) or so of vegetable or canola oil to rehydrate it.

CHOCOLATE CARAMEL PRETZEL COOKIE DOUGH

YIELD: SERVES 6 TO 8

This recipe pairs our classic rich chocolate dough with a gooey caramel sauce dotted with pretzels. It's crunchy, with an addicting sweet and salty flavor. It's a decadent enough dough to serve on Valentine's Day.

1. Place the pretzels into a resealable plastic bag and with a rolling pin or another heavy kitchen utensil, smash the pretzels up a bit. Don't do it so much that they turn into a powder, but just enough to get smaller bite-size pieces. Set aside.

2. In a medium saucepan, spread out the sugar so that it's evenly spread over the bottom of the pan. Begin to heat the sugar on high heat. After 30 seconds or so, start stirring the sugar. It should start to clump together as it begins to melt. That's okay; it's supposed to do that. The clumps will melt eventually.

3. Stir constantly as the sugar completely melts and begins to turn a light golden amber color. Caramel can go from perfect to burnt in a matter of a few seconds, so when you see that color, immediately add the butter. Be very careful because the caramel will boil up when the butter is added. Vigorously stir in the butter as it melts. Remove it from the heat as soon as the butter has been incorporated.

4. Add the cream. Again, be careful because the mixture may bubble up at you. Stir the caramel until all of the cream is incorporated and the caramel becomes smooth and shiny.

5. Add the pretzels and mix until all of them are coated in caramel. Don't be alarmed that the sauce is so thin. It will thicken and harden drastically as it cools.

6. Pour the finished caramel into a bowl and allow it cool completely before adding it to the dough and folding it in by hand.

7. Eat immediately or store in an airtight container for 1 month in the refrigerator or 3 months in the freezer.

1 cup (80 g) mini pretzels

½ cup (100 g) sugar

¼ cup (55 g) unsalted butter, softened

⅓ cup (80 ml) heavy cream

1 batch of Chocolate Cookie Dough (page 40)

SALTED CARAMEL COOKIE DOUGH

YIELD: SERVES 6 TO 8

This decadent dough is the perfect mix of sweet and salty. If you aren't a huge fan of the sweet-and-salty experience, simply omit the sea salt. Make sure to use the caramel pudding mix rather than real caramel sauce. I found that caramel sauce made the dough gummy in texture. Surprisingly, the caramel pudding mix tastes exactly like the real stuff. This recipe is perfect for dipping pretzels, too.

1. In the bowl of a stand mixer fitted with the paddle attachment, cream the butter and the sugars together until light and fluffy. It should take about 30 seconds on high. Scrape down the sides of the bowl when done.

2. In a small bowl, whisk together the flour, caramel pudding mix, and salt. Gradually add the flour mixture to the butter mixture. Mix on low until fully incorporated.

3. Add the caramel bits and fold them into the dough by hand until combined.

4. Add a sprinkle of sea salt on top when serving, if using.

5. Eat immediately or store in an airtight container for 2 weeks at room temperature, 1 month in the refrigerator, or 3 months in the freezer.

1 cup (225 g) unsalted butter, softened

½ cup (115 g) lightly packed brown sugar

¼ cup (50 g) granulated sugar

1½ cups (188 g) heat-treated all-purpose flour (page 15)

¼ cup plus 2 tablespoons (48 g) caramel pudding mix

¼ teaspoon coarse sea salt plus more for topping (optional)

½ cup (96 g) caramel bits (You can buy them at your local grocery store in the baking section. They look like small balls.)

PB&J COOKIE DOUGH

YIELD: SERVES 6 TO 8

I ate so many peanut butter sandwiches as a kid at school that I burned myself out on them for a few years. Thankfully, my love for them returned, and I knew I had to create this classic pairing in a cookie dough version. This dough will be loved by all PB&J fans. The recipe features a homemade strawberry jam, but if you prefer a different flavor of jam or jelly, just substitute it in.

1. Place the diced strawberries in a small bowl and mash them. I do this with a cocktail muddler, but a fork will do just fine if you don't have one. When you're done, you should have about ½ cup (85 g) of mashed berries.

2. In a medium saucepan, mix the strawberries, lemon juice, sugar, pectin, and salt together. Heat the mixture over medium-high heat until it begins to boil. Once it's at a full boil, allow it to boil for 2 minutes. Then, remove it from the heat and allow it to cool, about 30 minutes. It will thicken a lot as it cools, so don't be alarmed if the hot jam seems thin.

3. When the jam has cooled and is set, add it to the Peanut Butter Cookie Dough. Swirl the jam throughout the dough using a spoon.

4. Eat immediately or store in an airtight container for 1 month in the refrigerator or 3 months in the freezer.

¾ cup (128 g) diced strawberries

1 tablespoon (15 ml) lemon juice

¾ cup (150 g) sugar

½ teaspoon powdered pectin

Pinch of salt

1 batch of Peanut Butter Cookie Dough (page 71)

PEANUT BUTTER CUP COOKIE DOUGH

YIELD: SERVES 6 TO 8

Peanut butter cups are Alex's favorite candy. No matter the holiday, I buy him a bunch of them. He proceeds to eat them all, and then, when his stomach hurts, asks why I bought him so many. I feel like he should have some self-control, but obviously it's my fault. This dough is rich with peanut butter flavor, and the gooey sauce has an intense chocolate flavor.

1 To make the sauce, combine the sugar, water, and cocoa powder in a medium saucepan. Heat the mixture over medium-high heat until the mixture begins to fully boil, whisking occasionally. Once it's boiling, cook for another 1½ minutes without disturbing it. After that, immediately remove it from the heat. Don't be alarmed if the sauce seems too thin. It will thicken as it cools.

2. Add the peanut butter cups, peanut butter, and vanilla and stir until everything melts into the sauce.

3. Pour the sauce into a bowl, cover it with plastic wrap, and place it into the refrigerator to cool, about 30 minutes. Stir the sauce occasionally while it cools to break up the crust that will form on the top.

4. While the sauce cools, to make the cookie dough, cream the butter, peanut butter, and sugars together in the bowl of a stand mixer fitted with the paddle attachment until light and fluffy. It should take about 30 seconds on high. Scrape down the sides of the bowl when done.

5. Add the vanilla and mix until combined.

6. In a small bowl, whisk together the flour, cocoa powder, and salt. Gradually add the flour mixture to the butter mixture. Mix on low until the flour is fully incorporated.

7. Swirl in the cooled chocolate peanut butter sauce with a spoon.

8. Eat immediately or store in an airtight container for 2 weeks at room temperature, 1 month in the refrigerator, or 3 months in the freezer.

For chocolate peanut butter sauce:

½ cup (100 g) granulated sugar

¼ cup (60 ml) water

¼ cup (20 g) unsweetened cocoa powder

¼ cup (55 g) chopped peanut butter cups

1 tablespoon (16 g) creamy peanut butter

¼ teaspoon vanilla extract

For cookie dough:

¼ cup (112 g) unsalted butter, softened

½ cup (130 g) creamy peanut butter

¾ cup (170 g) lightly packed brown sugar

¼ cup (50 g) granulated sugar

¼ teaspoon vanilla extract

1¼ cups (156 g) heat-treated all-purpose flour (page 15)

1 tablespoon (5 g) unsweetened cocoa powder

⅛ teaspoon salt

NO-BAKE-COOKIE COOKIE DOUGH

YIELD: SERVES 6 TO 8

I was so excited to create this recipe to honor one of my favorite cookies to make, no-bake cookies. If you aren't familiar with the no-bake cookie, it's a cookie you make on the stovetop, and the main ingredients are peanut butter, cocoa powder, and oats. They are highly addicting, and I thought a dough version would be just as fantastic. And it is.

1. In the bowl of a stand mixer fitted with the paddle attachment, cream the butter, peanut butter, and sugar together until light and fluffy. It should take about 30 seconds on high. Scrape down the sides of the bowl when done.

2. In a medium bowl, whisk together the flour, oats, cocoa, and salt. Gradually add the flour mixture to the butter mixture. Mix on low until fully incorporated.

3. Eat immediately or store in an airtight container for 2 weeks at room temperature, 1 month in the refrigerator, or 3 months in the freezer.

¾ cup (167 g) unsalted butter, softened

½ cup (130 g) creamy peanut butter

1 cup (200 g) sugar

1¼ cups (156 g) heat-treated all-purpose flour (page 15)

1 cup (80 g) quick-cooking oats

¼ cup (20 g) unsweetened cocoa powder

¼ teaspoon salt

Note:
This dough is much less sweet than any of the other doughs, making it a nice choice for whenever you want something a little less sweet.

MONSTER COOKIE DOUGH

YIELD: SERVES 6 TO 8

Our MONSTER dough (yes, we always write it entirely in capital letters) is like the everything bagel. It has a little bit of everything in it to make it a dough that's sweet, salty, and full of flavor. This is my mom's favorite flavor and one I would never pass up either. If you don't like any of the toppings that are listed in the recipe, just switch them for a few of your favorites.

1. In the bowl of a stand mixer fitted with the paddle attachment, cream the butter, peanut butter, and sugars together until light and fluffy. It should take about 30 seconds on high. Scrape down the sides of the bowl when done.

2. Add the vanilla and mix until combined.

3. In a medium bowl, whisk together the flour, oats, and salt. Gradually add the flour mixture to the butter mixture. Mix on low until the flour is fully incorporated.

4. Fold the chocolate chips, M&M's, chocolate cookies, and rainbow sprinkles in by hand.

5. Eat immediately or store in an airtight container for 2 weeks at room temperature, 1 month in the refrigerator, or 3 months in the freezer.

Note:

If you don't have quick-cooking oats, simply take old-fashioned oats and pulse them in a blender or food processor. This will break down the oats into smaller pieces, resembling the texture of the quick-cooking oats.

½ cup (112 g) unsalted butter, softened

¾ cup (195 g) crunchy peanut butter

1 cup (225 g) lightly packed brown sugar

¼ cup (50 g) granulated sugar

½ teaspoon vanilla extract

1 cup (125 g) heat-treated all-purpose flour (page 15)

1 cup (80 g) quick-cooking oats

¼ teaspoon salt

½ cup (112 g) mini semisweet chocolate chips

½ cup (85 g) mini M&M's

½ cup (40 g) chopped chocolate sandwich cookies

¼ cup (30 g) rainbow sprinkles

'THE ELVIS' COOKIE DOUGH

YIELD: SERVES 6 TO 8

If Elvis ever ate edible cookie dough, it 100 percent tasted like this. It's a take on his favorite sandwich, which included peanut butter, bananas, and bacon. This dough is full of peanut butter and banana flavor, and the bits of bacon give it a great crunch. It's just as delicious (well, almost as delicious) without the bacon, if you prefer to leave it out. Spread this on two pieces of bread to eat the cookie dough version of the King's popular sandwich!

1. In a medium skillet, cook the bacon on medium heat until mildly crunchy (feel free to make it more or less crunchy to fit your liking). Once cooked, place it on paper towels to drain and cool. Set aside.

2. In a small bowl, mash the banana with a fork until smooth. Set aside.

3. In the bowl of a stand mixer fitted with the paddle attachment, cream the butter, peanut butter, and the sugars together until light and fluffy. It should take about 30 seconds on high. Scrape down the sides of the bowl when done.

4. Add the banana and mix until incorporated. Then, add the vanilla and mix until combined.

5. In a small bowl, whisk together the flour and salt. Gradually add the flour mixture to the butter mixture. Mix on low until the flour is fully incorporated.

6. Add the cooked bacon to the dough, mixing on low until fully incorporated.

7. Eat immediately or store in an airtight container for 5 days in the refrigerator or 2 weeks in the freezer.

2 strips of thick-cut bacon

½ of a large very ripe banana

½ cup (112 g) unsalted butter, softened

½ cup (130 g) creamy peanut butter

½ cup (115 g) lightly packed brown sugar

½ cup (100 g) granulated sugar

½ teaspoon vanilla extract

1½ cups (188 g) heat-treated all-purpose flour (page 15)

⅛ teaspoon salt

BANANA PUDDING COOKIE DOUGH

YIELD: SERVES 6 TO 8

This genius flavor idea was thought up by a friend of mine, Nick. I was so excited when he brought it to my attention. I eagerly tested it out, and after some trial and error, this recipe was born. Make sure to use an all-natural banana-flavored pudding mix. One of my errors was using an artificially flavored mix. Jell-O has a new line of all-natural mixes called Simply Good, which work perfectly.

1. Place the vanilla wafers in a resealable plastic bag and make sure the bag is closed with most of the air out of it. With a rolling pin or another heavy kitchen utensil, smash the cookies until medium crumbs form. Set aside.

2. In the bowl of a stand mixer fitted with the paddle attachment, cream the butter and sugar together until light and fluffy. It should take about 30 seconds on high. Scrape down the sides of the bowl when done.

3. Add the vanilla and mix on low until combined.

4. In a small bowl, whisk together the flour, pudding mix, and salt. Gradually add the flour mixture to the butter mixture. Mix on low until fully incorporated.

5. Add the food coloring until the dough turns a very light tint of yellow. If you prefer a brighter yellow, continue to add drops of coloring until your desired color is reached.

6. Add the crushed cookies to the dough and fold in by hand.

7. Eat immediately or store in an airtight container for 2 weeks at room temperature, 1 month in the refrigerator, or 3 months in the freezer.

12 vanilla wafer cookies

1 cup (225 g) unsalted butter, softened

1 cup (200 g) sugar

½ teaspoon vanilla extract

1½ cups (188 g) heat-treated all-purpose flour (page 15)

¼ cup (32 g) banana pudding mix

¼ teaspoon salt

6 to 8 drops yellow food coloring

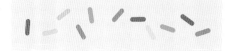

OATMEAL COOKIE DOUGH

YIELD: SERVES 6 TO 8

This dough will take you back to Grandma's house. It's full of wonderful warm spices, and the oats give it a great texture. If you prefer a spicier dough, add more cinnamon and nutmeg or an additional spice, like ground ginger. This recipe, of course, pairs great with raisins. My personal favorite topping for this dough, though, is butterscotch chips. If you've never tried this pairing before, give it a shot. It's fantastic!

1. In the bowl of a stand mixer fitted with the paddle attachment, cream the butter and the sugars together until light and fluffy. It should take about 30 seconds on high. Scrape down the sides of the bowl when done.

2. Add the vanilla and mix until combined.

3. In a medium bowl, whisk together the flour, oats, cinnamon, nutmeg, and salt. Gradually add the flour mixture to the butter mixture. Mix on low until the flour is fully incorporated.

4. Eat immediately or store in an airtight container for 2 weeks at room temperature, 1 month in the refrigerator, or 3 months in the freezer.

1 cup (225 g) unsalted butter, softened

1 cup (225 g) lightly packed brown sugar

¼ cup (50 g) granulated sugar

½ teaspoon vanilla extract

1¼ cups (156 g) heat-treated all-purpose flour (page 15)

1 cup (80 g) quick-cooking oats

1 teaspoon ground cinnamon

¼ teaspoon ground nutmeg

⅛ teaspoon salt

SNICKERDOODLE COOKIE DOUGH

YIELD: SERVES 6 TO 8

This is a delicious and simple recipe that, dare I say, is good for breakfast! It has a strong cinnamon flavor that will intensify over time. It makes a great spread for a bagel, or just indulge in a scoop with a cup of coffee.

1. In the bowl of a stand mixer fitted with the paddle attachment, cream the butter and the sugars together until light and fluffy. It should take about 30 seconds on high. Scrape down the sides of the bowl when done.

2. Add the vanilla and mix until combined.

3. In a small bowl, whisk together the flour, cinnamon, and salt. Gradually add the flour mixture to the butter mixture. Mix on low until the flour is fully incorporated.

4. Eat immediately or store in an airtight container for 2 weeks at room temperature, 1 month in the refrigerator, or 3 months in the freezer.

1 cup (225 g) unsalted butter, softened

1 cup (225 g) lightly packed brown sugar

¼ cup (50 g) granulated sugar

½ teaspoon vanilla extract

1¾ cups (220 g) heat-treated all-purpose flour (page 15)

1½ teaspoons ground cinnamon

⅛ teaspoon salt

NUTELLA CHURRO COOKIE DOUGH

YIELD: SERVES 6 TO 8

This flavor combo came from one of Unbaked's very first customers, Naz, in a flavor competition we held. It has been one of our most popular flavors ever since! It's rich with cinnamon sugar flavor, and the Nutella adds a creamy, nutty taste.

1. In a food processor or blender, grind the cereal up into fine crumbs. Make them as fine as you can and then set them aside.

2. In the bowl of a stand mixer fitted with the paddle attachment, cream the butter and the sugars together until light and fluffy. It should take about 30 seconds on high. Scrape down the sides of the bowl when done.

3. Add the vanilla and mix until combined.

4. In a medium bowl, whisk together the flour, cinnamon, salt, and reserved cereal crumbs. Gradually add the flour mixture to the butter mixture. Mix on low until the flour is fully incorporated.

5. Fold in the chocolate chips by hand and then swirl in the Nutella using a spoon so that you have streaks of it running through the dough.

6. Eat immediately or store in an airtight container for 2 weeks at room temperature, 1 month in the refrigerator, or 3 months in the freezer.

1½ cups (65 g) cinnamon crunch cereal

1 cup (225 g) unsalted butter, softened

½ cup (115 g) lightly packed brown sugar

¼ cup (50 g) granulated sugar

¼ teaspoon vanilla extract

1¼ cups (156 g) heat-treated all-purpose flour (page 15)

¾ teaspoon ground cinnamon

⅛ teaspoon salt

½ cup (112 g) mini semisweet chocolate chips

½ cup (148 g) Nutella

COOKIES 'N' CREAM COOKIE DOUGH

YIELD: SERVES 6 TO 8

This dough is a great traditional flavor, and it's one of our top three most popular on UnbakedBar.com. It has a strong vanilla flavor, and the cookies give it a great crunch. Try this dough in between two ice cream sandwiches. You'll make a mess, but it's so worth it.

1. First, decide how many chocolate sandwich cookies you want to use. If you want a dough with bigger chunks and more cookie flavor, use 10. If you want a dough with smaller chunks and more of a cream flavor, use 8. Place the cookies into a large resealable plastic bag and seal it with almost no air in it. Using a rolling pin or another heavy kitchen utensil, smash the bag to break up the cookies. You can choose to smash them into large pieces or a fine dust. It's up to you. Once done, set them aside.

2. In the bowl of a stand mixer fitted with the paddle attachment, cream the butter and sugar together until light and fluffy. It should take about 30 seconds on high. Scrape down the sides of the bowl when done.

3. Add the vanilla and mix until combined.

4. In a small bowl, whisk together the flour and salt. Gradually add the flour mixture to the butter mixture. Mix on low until the flour is fully incorporated.

5. Gently fold in the cookie pieces by hand.

6. Eat immediately or store in an airtight container for 2 weeks at room temperature, 1 month in the refrigerator, or 3 months in the freezer.

8 to 10 chocolate sandwich cookies

1 cup (225 g) unsalted butter, softened

1 cup (200 g) sugar

1 teaspoon vanilla extract

1½ cups (188 g) heat-treated all-purpose flour (page 15)

¼ teaspoon salt

Note:
Easily make this recipe into a Winter Edition by swapping out the regular chocolate sandwich cookies for mint ones. You will get a subtle mint flavor that is perfect for the holidays! For more variations, feel free to use any flavored chocolate sandwich cookie you'd like.

FLUFFERNUTTER COOKIE DOUGH

YIELD: SERVES 6 TO 8

This old-fashioned flavor is a fun take on the fluffernutter sandwich. I have personally never had a traditional fluffernutter sandwich, but I have had this dough spread on two pieces of bread. And boy oh boy, is it yummy!

1. In the bowl of a stand mixer fitted with the paddle attachment, cream the butter, peanut butter, and the sugars together until light and fluffy. It should take about 30 seconds on high. Scrape down the sides of the bowl when done.

2. Add ¼ cup (24 g) of the marshmallow creme and mix until fully combined. Then, add the vanilla and mix.

3. In a small bowl, whisk together the flour and salt. Gradually add the flour mixture to the butter mixture. Mix on low until the flour is fully incorporated.

4. Swirl the remaining ½ cup (48 g) of marshmallow creme throughout the dough using a spoon.

5. Eat immediately or store in an airtight container for 2 weeks at room temperature, 1 month in the refrigerator, or 3 months in the freezer.

¾ cup (167 g) unsalted butter, softened

¼ cup (65 g) creamy peanut butter

½ cup (115 g) lightly packed brown sugar

¼ cup (50 g) granulated sugar

¾ cup (72 g) marshmallow creme

¼ teaspoon vanilla extract

1½ cups (188 g) heat-treated all-purpose flour (page 15)

⅛ teaspoon salt

PEANUT BUTTER COOKIE DOUGH

YIELD: SERVES 6 TO 8

If you love peanut butter, you will adore this dough. It's rich and full of peanut butter flavor. It's also the perfect dough for anyone who doesn't like overly sweet desserts since the peanut butter keeps the sweetness down and adds a touch of saltiness. When whipping this dough up, do just that: Whip it. Make sure the peanut butter and sugars are whipped until very light and fluffy. It makes all the difference. If you are a fan of crunchy peanut butter, feel free to swap it for the creamy peanut butter. It will give you a wonderful crunchy texture!

1. In the bowl of a stand mixer fitted with the paddle attachment, cream the peanut butter, butter, and the sugars together until light and fluffy. It should take about 30 seconds on high. The color of the mixture should lighten significantly after whipping. Scrape down the sides of the bowl when done.

2. Add the vanilla and mix on low until combined.

3. In a small bowl, whisk together the flour and salt. Gradually add the flour mixture to the peanut butter mixture, mixing on low until fully incorporated.

4. Eat immediately or store in an airtight container for 2 weeks at room temperature, 1 month in the refrigerator, or 3 months in the freezer.

½ cup (130 g) creamy peanut butter

½ cup (112 g) unsalted butter, softened

¾ cup (170 g) lightly packed brown sugar

¼ cup (50 g) granulated sugar

¼ teaspoon vanilla extract

1 cup (125 g) heat-treated all-purpose flour (page 15)

¼ teaspoon salt

MINT CHOCOLATE CHIP COOKIE DOUGH

YIELD: SERVES 6 TO 8

Mint chocolate chip is one of my dad's favorite ice cream flavors. This dough tastes exactly like the real stuff! My dad, who isn't even a cookie dough fan (I know, he's crazy), loves this flavor. It has the perfect amount of mint to tingle your taste buds, but it isn't overpowering. The dough would go great on top of vanilla ice cream or cookies 'n' cream ice cream. If you are a dark chocolate fan, try swapping the semisweet chips for dark chocolate chips.

1. In the bowl of a stand mixer fitted with the paddle attachment, cream the butter and sugar together until light and fluffy. It should take about 30 seconds on high. Scrape down the sides of the bowl when done.

2. Add the peppermint extract and mix until combined.

3. In a small bowl, whisk together the flour and salt. Gradually add the flour mixture to the butter mixture. Mix on low until the flour is fully incorporated. Add the food coloring and mix until the dough turns green. If you want a deeper green color, just add more food coloring.

4. Fold in the chocolate chips by hand.

5. Eat immediately or store in an airtight container for 2 weeks at room temperature, 1 month in the refrigerator, or 3 months in the freezer.

1 cup (225 g) unsalted butter, softened

1 cup (200 g) sugar

½ teaspoon peppermint extract

1¾ cups (220 g) heat-treated all-purpose flour (page 15)

⅛ teaspoon salt

¼ teaspoon green food coloring

½ cup (88 g) semisweet chocolate chips

GRAHAM CRACKER COOKIE DOUGH

YIELD: SERVES 6 TO 8

My mom loves graham crackers and used to buy graham cracker frozen yogurt. I figured I would try to make this in dough form, and it really turned out great. It tastes just like . . . wait for it . . . a graham cracker! The dough has a slightly grainier texture than others, but this adds to the real graham cracker taste. Add some chocolate chips and mini marshmallows to make this into a delicious s'mores dough.

1. In a food processor or blender, grind the graham crackers until a very fine powder forms. You can do this by hand by placing the crackers in a resealable plastic bag, but it may result in a grainier dough, as the crumbs won't be as fine. Set aside.

2. In the bowl of a stand mixer fitted with the paddle attachment, cream the butter and the sugars together until light and fluffy. It should take about 30 seconds on high. Scrape down the sides of the bowl when done.

3. Add the vanilla and mix until combined.

4. In a small bowl, whisk together the flour, salt, and the graham cracker crumbs. Gradually add the flour mixture to the butter mixture. Mix on low until fully incorporated.

5. Eat immediately or store in an airtight container for 2 weeks at room temperature, 1 month in the refrigerator, or 3 months in the freezer.

8 full-size graham crackers

1 cup (225 g) unsalted butter, softened

¾ cup (170 g) lightly packed brown sugar

¼ cup (50 g) granulated sugar

½ teaspoon vanilla extract

1½ cups (188 g) heat-treated all-purpose flour (page 15)

¼ teaspoon salt

CARAMEL MACCHIATO COOKIE DOUGH

YIELD: SERVES 6 TO 8

Eating this dough will transport you to a little coffee shop in Europe. It has the perfect balance of both strong coffee and caramel tastes. You really do get a pop of each flavor in your mouth, with the coffee coming first and the sweet caramel on the back end. Add some chocolate chips to create an even more decadent flavor pairing. This would be fun to serve at a family brunch.

1. In the bowl of a stand mixer fitted with the paddle attachment, cream the butter and the sugars together until light and fluffy. It should take about 30 seconds on high. Scrape down the sides of the bowl when done.

2. Add the instant coffee powder and mix until combined.

3. In a small bowl, whisk together the flour, pudding mix, and salt. Gradually add the flour mixture to the butter mixture. Mix on low until the flour is fully incorporated.

4. Eat immediately or store in an airtight container for 2 weeks at room temperature, 1 month in the refrigerator, or 3 months in the freezer.

1 cup (225 g) unsalted butter, softened

½ cup (115 g) lightly packed brown sugar

⅓ cup (67 g) granulated sugar

2 teaspoons instant coffee powder

1½ cups (188 g) heat-treated all-purpose flour (page 15)

½ cup (32 g) caramel pudding mix

⅛ teaspoon salt

COFFEE COOKIE DOUGH

YIELD: SERVES 6 TO 8

If you love coffee, you will be obsessed with this dough. It would be perfect as a spread on a scone in the morning. I personally like a more subtle coffee taste. If you prefer a stronger coffee flavor, feel free to add more instant coffee. It will give you more of that traditional bitter coffee taste.

1. In the bowl of a stand mixer fitted with the paddle attachment, cream the butter and the sugars together until light and fluffy. It should take about 30 seconds on high. Scrape down the sides of the bowl when done.

2. Add the vanilla and mix until combined.

3. In a small bowl, whisk together the flour, instant coffee powder, and salt. Gradually add the flour mixture to the butter mixture. Mix on low until fully incorporated.

4. Eat immediately or store in an airtight container for 2 weeks at room temperature, 1 month in the refrigerator, or 3 months in the freezer.

1 cup (225 g) unsalted butter, softened

½ cup (115 g) lightly packed brown sugar

½ cup (100 g) granulated sugar

½ teaspoon vanilla extract

1¾ cups (220 g) heat-treated all-purpose flour (page 15)

1 tablespoon plus 1 teaspoon (4 g) instant coffee powder

¼ teaspoon salt

CHEESECAKE COOKIE DOUGH

YIELD: SERVES 6 TO 8

I'm such a big fan of cheesecake that I used to have it as my birthday cake when I was a kid. Naturally, I knew I had to create a cookie dough version, and this one really does taste like cheesecake. It has a wonderful tang to it and is not overly sweet. Swirl some cherry pie filling throughout the dough, if you like, to create a classic cherry cheesecake flaovr.

1. Place the graham crackers in a resealable plastic bag and seal it with most of the air out of it. Using a rolling pin or another heavy kitchen utensil, smash the crackers until fine crumbs form. Smash the crackers less if you want bigger chunks in your dough. Set aside.

2. In the bowl of a stand mixer fitted with the paddle attachment, cream the butter, cream cheese, and sugar together until fully incorporated. It should take about 30 seconds on high. It won't get as fluffy as other doughs due to the density of the cream cheese. Scrape down the sides of the bowl when done.

3. Add the vanilla and mix until combined.

4. In a small bowl, whisk together the flour and salt. Gradually add the flour mixture to the butter mixture. Mix on low until the flour is fully incorporated.

5. Fold in the graham cracker crumbs by hand.

6. Eat immediately or store in an airtight container for 1 month in the refrigerator or 3 months in the freezer.

2 full-size graham crackers

½ cup (112 g) unsalted butter, softened

6 ounces (170 g) cream cheese, softened

½ cup (100 g) sugar

1 teaspoon vanilla extract

1½ cups (188 g) heat-treated all-purpose flour (page 15)

¼ teaspoon salt

MUD PIE COOKIE DOUGH

YIELD: SERVES 6 TO 8

I love mud pie and always order it when I go to my favorite restaurant in San Diego, where I'm from. This dough has a punch of coffee flavor and a lovely crunch from the peanuts. Serve this on top of ice cream with whipped cream for the full mud pie experience.

1. To make the syrup, combine the sugar, water, and cocoa powder in a medium saucepan. Heat the mixture over medium-high heat until the mixture begins to fully boil, whisking occasionally. Once it's boiling, cook for another 1½ minutes without disturbing it. After that, immediately remove it from the heat. Don't be alarmed if the sauce seems too thin. It will thicken as it cools, so don't overboil it or it will turn into a paste.

2. Stir in the vanilla and then pour the syrup into a bowl. Cover and allow it to chill in the refrigerator until cool, about 30 minutes. Stir the syrup occasionally while it cools to break up the crust that will form on the top.

3. While the syrup chills, to make the cookie dough, cream the butter and the sugars together in the bowl of a stand mixer fitted with the paddle attachment until light and fluffy. It should take about 30 seconds on high. Scrape down the sides of the bowl when done.

4. Add the vanilla and mix until combined. Then, add the cookie crumbs and instant coffee powder and mix until combined.

5. In a small bowl, whisk together the flour and salt. Gradually add the flour mixture to the butter mixture. Mix on low until the flour is fully incorporated.

6. If you are using the peanuts, fold them in by hand. Add the chocolate syrup and swirl it throughout the dough using a spoon.

7. Eat immediately or store in an airtight container for 2 weeks at room temperature, 1 month in the refrigerator, or 3 months in the freezer.

For chocolate syrup:

½ cup (100 g) sugar

¼ cup (60 ml) water

¼ cup (20 g) unsweetened cocoa powder

¼ teaspoon vanilla extract

For cookie dough:

1 cup (225 g) unsalted butter, softened

½ cup (115 g) lightly packed brown sugar

½ cup (100 g) granulated sugar

½ teaspoon vanilla extract

2 tablespoons (10 g) fine chocolate sandwich cookie crumbs

1 tablespoon plus 1 teaspoon (4 g) instant coffee powder

1½ cups (188 g) heat-treated all-purpose flour (page 15)

⅛ teaspoon salt

⅓ cup (48 g) chopped peanuts (optional)

TIRAMISU COOKIE DOUGH

YIELD: SERVES 6 TO 8

Tiramisu is Alex's favorite dessert, and he approves of this dough version of the Italian treat. It's extra creamy from the mascarpone cheese, and the instant coffee adds its signature strong and pleasantly bitter coffee taste. Add some big chunks of leftover ladyfingers, if you like. It will give the dough a nice textural contrast and make you feel like you're eating real tiramisu at a fancy Italian restaurant.

1. In a food processor or blender, grind the ladyfingers into very fine crumbs. Make them as fine as you can get them. You should get about ½ cup (40 g) of crumbs. If you are short, grind up a few more cookies and then set them all aside.

2. In the bowl of a stand mixer fitted with the paddle attachment, combine the butter and mascarpone until smooth. Add the sugar and cream until light and fluffy. It should take about 30 seconds on high. Scrape down the sides of the bowl when done.

3. Add the vanilla and mix until combined. Then, add the ladyfingers and mix on low until incorporated.

4. In a small bowl, whisk together the flour, instant coffee powder, cocoa powder, and salt. Gradually add the flour mixture to the butter mixture. Mix on low until the flour is fully incorporated.

5. Eat immediately or store in an airtight container for 1 month in the refrigerator or 3 months in the freezer.

6 ladyfingers

¾ cup (167 g) unsalted butter, softened

½ cup (120 g) mascarpone cheese

¾ cup (150 g) sugar

¼ teaspoon vanilla extract

1 cup (125 g) heat-treated all-purpose flour (page 15)

1 tablespoon (3 g) instant coffee powder

2 teaspoons unsweetened cocoa powder

⅛ teaspoon salt

CANNOLI COOKIE DOUGH

YIELD: SERVES 6 TO 8

Whenever I think about cannoli, I think of my aunt Janet. She's a hoot, and when I was visiting New York City with my mom for the first time, she drove up from Philadelphia to see us. We went to Little Italy just so she could find a cannoli shop. Well, she did, and she just about wiped the entire store clean of the Italian treats. The story makes me laugh, and it's one I will never forget. This dough is dedicated to her! If you want to create some cannoli-ception, fill cannoli shells with this dough.

1. Place the ice cream cones into a resealable plastic bag and seal with most of the air out of it. Using a rolling pin or another heavy kitchen utensil, smash the cones into small pieces. Set aside.

2. In the bowl of a stand mixer fitted with the paddle attachment, combine the butter and ricotta until smooth. Add the sugar and cream until light and fluffy. It should take about 30 seconds on high. Scrape down the sides of the bowl when done.

3. Add the vanilla and mix until combined. If you're using the lemon zest, add it and mix until combined.

4. In a small bowl, whisk together the flour and salt. Gradually add the flour mixture to the butter mixture. Mix on low until the flour is fully incorporated.

5. Fold in the chocolate chips and the sugar cone pieces by hand.

6. Eat immediately or store in an airtight container for 1 month in the refrigerator or 3 months in the freezer.

2 sugar ice cream cones

¾ cup (167 g) unsalted butter, softened

¾ cup (188 g) whole-milk ricotta cheese

½ cup (100 g) sugar

½ teaspoon vanilla extract

½ teaspoon lemon zest (optional)

1½ cups (188 g) heat-treated all-purpose flour (page 15)

⅛ teaspoon salt

½ cup (88 g) mini semisweet chocolate chips

VANILLA BEAN COOKIE DOUGH

YIELD: SERVES 6 TO 8

This dough isn't just a simple sugar cookie dough—it's a true vanilla bean cookie dough. By incorporating real vanilla beans and vanilla bean paste, this dough gets packed with strong vanilla flavor. It tastes like a velvety vanilla bean ice cream. The only difference is, it's not cold!

1. First, to extract the seeds from the vanilla bean, slice the bean open down the middle. Using the back of a small knife, carefully slide it down the cut part of the vanilla bean, separating the pod from the seeds. You'll be left with a cluster of little black seeds and an empty pod. Set the seeds aside and reserve.

2. Place the empty vanilla pod and the sugar in a food processor and grind the vanilla pod into the sugar. The pods are tough, so it won't completely break down. You will most likely still have chunks of the pod in the sugar, but that's okay.

3. Sift the sugar into the bowl of a stand mixer. This will eliminate the big chunks of leftover pod and leave you with a vanilla sugar.

4. Add the butter to the mixer and using the paddle attachment, cream the butter with the vanilla sugar until light and fluffy. It should take about 30 seconds on high. Scrape down the sides of the bowl when done.

5. Add the reserved vanilla bean seeds and the vanilla bean paste to the butter and mix until combined.

6. In a small bowl, whisk together the flour and salt. Gradually add the flour mixture to the butter mixture. Mix on low until the flour is fully incorporated.

7. Eat immediately or store in an airtight container for 2 weeks at room temperature, 1 month in the refrigerator, or 3 months in the freezer.

1 vanilla bean

1 cup (200 g) sugar

1 cup (225 g) unsalted butter, softened

2 teaspoons vanilla bean paste

2 cups (250 g) heat-treated all-purpose flour (page 15)

⅛ teaspoon salt

FROSTED ANIMAL COOKIES COOKIE DOUGH

YIELD: SERVES 6 TO 8

I grew up snacking on those cute frosted pink and white animal cookies with sprinkles. They are a fun memory for a lot of kids (and adults), and this dough will bring you right back to those times. This nostalgic dough is full of animal cookie flavor as is, but add some big chunks of cookies and some nonpareils or sprinkles to make it even more fun. The dough is a beautiful light pink color, like the cookies, and would be a perfect summertime snack!

30 frosted animal cookies, such as Mother's Circus Animal Cookies

1 cup (225 g) unsalted butter, softened

¾ cup (150 g) sugar

¼ teaspoon vanilla extract

1¾ cups (220 g) heat-treated all-purpose flour (page 15)

⅛ teaspoon salt

1. In a food processor or blender, grind the animal cookies to very fine crumbs. Make them as fine as you can get them. You should get about 1 cup (80 g) of crumbs. If you are short, grind up a few more cookies and then set them all aside.

2. In the bowl of a stand mixer fitted with the paddle attachment, cream the butter and sugar together until light and fluffy. It should take about 30 seconds on high. Scrape down the sides of the bowl when done.

3. Add the cookie crumbs and beat on high for another 30 seconds or so. Add the vanilla and mix until combined.

4. In a small bowl, whisk together the flour and salt. Gradually add the flour mixture to the butter mixture. Mix on low until the flour is fully incorporated.

5. Eat immediately or store in an airtight container for 2 weeks at room temperature, 1 month in the refrigerator, or 3 months in the freezer.

UNICORN COOKIE DOUGH

YIELD: SERVES 6 TO 8

This unicorn dough is super fun and full of bright colors. The flavor of the dough is creamy vanilla and sweet strawberry. It's perfect for a birthday party or other celebration. It's also a great dough to let the kiddos help you with. They'll have a blast coloring each of the doughs and adding the "sparkly" sprinkles. For a fancy touch, add some edible gold glitter to the top of the dough.

1. In the bowl of a stand mixer fitted with the paddle attachment, cream the butter and granulated sugar together until light and fluffy. It should take about 30 seconds on high. Scrape down the sides of the bowl when done.

2. Add the vanilla and mix until combined.

3. In a small bowl, whisk together the flour and salt. Gradually add the flour mixture to the butter mixture. Mix on low until the flour is fully incorporated.

4. Separate ½ cup (120 ml) of the dough into a medium bowl. Add the strawberry cake mix and mix until combined.

5. Back in the mixer bowl, add the white cake mix and mix until combined.

6. Separate the white cake dough into three equal parts in separate small bowls. Add the blue, yellow, and purple food coloring to each of the doughs, one color in each bowl, and mix until fully incorporated.

7. Add the hot pink food coloring to the strawberry dough and mix. Add the sanding sugar to the strawberry dough and mix.

8. Transfer all of the four colored dough to a large bowl. Gently swirl the colors together by hand to form a colorful rainbow dough. Be sure not to overmix at this point, or you'll end up with a dough that is all one color: muddy. Not pretty!

9. Eat immediately or store in an airtight container for 2 weeks at room temperature, 1 month in the refrigerator, or 3 months in the freezer.

1¼ cups (280 g) unsalted butter, softened

1 cup (200 g) granulated sugar

¼ teaspoon vanilla extract

1 cup (125 g) heat-treated all-purpose flour (page 15)

⅛ teaspoon salt

½ cup (63 g) strawberry cake mix

1 cup (125 g) white cake mix

¼ teaspoon blue food coloring

¼ teaspoon yellow food coloring

¼ teaspoon purple food coloring

¼ teaspoon hot pink food coloring

2 tablespoons (28 g) hot pink sanding sugar

PINK LEMONADE COOKIE DOUGH

YIELD: SERVES 6 TO 8

This dough is absolutely fantastic and one of my favorite new flavors. It brings me back to my childhood because it tastes like a certain brand of push-up pops I used to eat. I can't recommend this dough enough. It's a beautiful pink color and has a gentle kick of tartness. It's great for kids on a hot summer day by the pool.

1. In the bowl of a stand mixer fitted with the paddle attachment, cream the butter and sugar together until light and fluffy. It should take about 30 seconds on high. Scrape down the sides of the bowl when done.

2. Add the lemon zest and lemon juice to the butter mixture and mix until combined.

3. In a small bowl, whisk together the flour, gelatin powder, and salt. Gradually add the flour mixture to the butter mixture. Mix on low until the flour is fully incorporated.

4. Eat immediately or store in an airtight container for 2 weeks at room temperature, 1 month in the refrigerator, or 3 months in the freezer.

1 cup (225 g) unsalted butter, softened

1 cup (200 g) sugar

Zest of 1 lemon

1 tablespoon (15 ml) lemon juice

1½ cups (188 g) heat-treated all-purpose flour (page 15)

2 tablespoons (14 g) strawberry gelatin powder

¼ teaspoon salt

STRAWBERRIES AND CREAM COOKIE DOUGH

YIELD: SERVES 6 TO 8

This dough is full of real strawberry flavor, and that's what makes it so delicious. Homemade strawberry jam gives the dough a true fresh strawberry flavor instead of an artificial one. The vanilla bean paste adds a beautiful vanilla undertone that gives the strawberry flavor its "cream" counterpart.

1. In the bowl of a stand mixer fitted with the paddle attachment, cream the butter and sugar together until light and fluffy. It should take about 30 seconds on high. Scrape down the sides of the bowl when done.

2. Add the vanilla bean paste to the butter mixture and mix until combined.

3. In a medium bowl, whisk together the flour and salt. Gradually add the flour mixture to the butter mixture. Mix on low until the flour is fully incorporated.

4. Gently swirl the jam throughout the dough with a spoon.

5. Eat immediately or store in an airtight container for 1 month in the refrigerator or 3 months in the freezer.

1 cup (225 g) unsalted butter, softened

1 cup (200 g) sugar

1 teaspoon vanilla bean paste

2¼ cups (282 g) heat-treated all-purpose flour (page 15)

⅛ teaspoon salt

1 batch of strawberry jam (see page 54)

KAHLÚA COOKIE DOUGH

YIELD: SERVES 6 TO 8

Since turning 21, I've been on a mission to figure out what my favorite alcoholic beverages are. As it turns out, there isn't much I like. So far, Kahlúa and cream is the only drink (besides a strawberry daiquiri) that I can manage. Kahlúa has a beautiful coffee flavor, and I just knew it would make a delicious boozy cookie dough. If you aren't a fan of Kahlúa or like another liqueur better, feel free to make a swap.

1. In the bowl of a stand mixer fitted with the paddle attachment, cream the butter and sugar together until light and fluffy. It should take about 30 seconds on high. Scrape down the sides of the bowl when done.

2. Add the Kahlúa and vanilla and mix until combined.

3. In a medium bowl, whisk together the flour, instant coffee powder, and salt. Gradually add the flour mixture to the butter mixture. Mix on low until fully incorporated.

4. Eat immediately or store in an airtight container for 1 month in the refrigerator or 3 months in the freezer.

1 cup (225 g) unsalted butter, softened

1 cup (200 g) sugar

½ cup plus 2 tablespoons (148 ml) Kahlúa

¼ teaspoon vanilla extract

2½ cups (313 g) heat-treated all-purpose flour (page 15)

½ teaspoon instant coffee powder

¼ teaspoon salt

STRAWBERRY COCONUT DAIQUIRI COOKIE DOUGH

YIELD: SERVES 6 TO 8

Since the only alcoholic drink I like other than Kahlúa and cream is a strawberry daiquiri, I felt I had to turn that into a boozy cookie dough, too. I used coconut-flavored rum to give the dough an extra layer of flavor. If you don't like coconut, feel free to use regular rum.

1. In the bowl of a stand mixer fitted with the paddle attachment, cream the butter and sugar together until light and fluffy. It should take about 30 seconds on high. Scrape down the sides of the bowl when done.

2. Add the lime zest, lime juice, and rum and mix until combined.

3. In a medium bowl, whisk together the flour, gelatin powder, and salt. Gradually add the flour mixture to the butter mixture. Mix on low until fully incorporated.

4. Eat immediately or store in an airtight container for 1 month in the refrigerator or 3 months in the freezer.

1 cup (225 g) unsalted butter, softened

⅔ cup (133 g) sugar

½ teaspoon lime zest

2 teaspoons lime juice

¼ cup (60 ml) coconut rum

2¼ cups (281 g) heat-treated all-purpose flour (page 15)

1 tablespoon (7 g) strawberry gelatin powder

⅛ teaspoon salt

EGGNOG COOKIE DOUGH

YIELD: SERVES 6 TO 8

This dough is a wonderful and creative dessert to serve at all your holiday parties. It incorporates real eggnog, and by grating your own fresh nutmeg (use a Microplane), you get a powerful kick of this warm spice. There is alcohol in this dough, but if you want to serve it to kids, just omit the rum. Or, if you prefer a different alcohol in your eggnog, you can easily switch the rum for your spirit of choice.

1. To make the eggnog cream, whisk together the egg yolk and cream in a medium bowl. Set aside.

2. In a medium saucepan over medium-high heat, bring the milk and sugar to a simmer. Make sure to whisk the mixture frequently.

3. When it's simmering, pour about ½ cup (120 ml) of the hot liquid into the egg and cream mixture. Whisk continuously and vigorously while doing this. The goal is to temper the egg so that it can be heated on the stovetop. If you don't do this step or don't whisk while adding the hot milk, you will end up with scrambled eggs! Once the egg mixture is tempered, pour it into the remaining milk in the medium saucepan and return it to medium-high heat.

4. Add the rum and vanilla to the mixture and whisk until combined. Stir the nutmeg into the mixture. Allow the mixture to simmer and thicken while whisking constantly. It should take about 5 minutes to become a thick cream. You'll know it's ready when it sticks to the back of a spoon and you can run your finger and create a line down the middle. When thickened, pour into a bowl. Cover it with plastic wrap and place it in the refrigerator to cool, about 20 minutes.

5. While the cream cools, to make the cookie dough, cream the butter and sugar together in the bowl of a stand mixer fitted with the paddle attachment until light and fluffy. It should take about 30 seconds on high. Scrape down the sides of the bowl when done.

6. Add the cooled eggnog cream and rum and mix.

For eggnog cream:

1 egg yolk

½ cup (120 ml) heavy cream

½ cup (120 ml) milk

1 tablespoon (13 g) sugar

1 teaspoon rum

⅛ teaspoon vanilla extract

⅛ teaspoon freshly grated nutmeg

For cookie dough:

1 cup (225 g) unsalted butter, softened

1 cup (200 g) sugar

½ cup (120 ml) eggnog cream (see above)

2 tablespoons (28 ml) rum

2¼ cups (282 g) heat-treated all-purpose flour (page 15)

⅛ teaspoon freshly grated nutmeg

⅛ teaspoon salt

7. In a medium bowl, whisk together the flour, nutmeg, and salt. Gradually add the flour mixture to the butter mixture. Mix on low until the flour is fully incorporated.

8. Eat immediately or store in an airtight container for 1 month in the refrigerator or 3 months in the freezer.

Notes:

If you don't have fresh whole nutmeg, simply substitute ground nutmeg. Keep in mind that fresh nutmeg is stronger than its ground counterpart, so you may need to add slightly more of the ground spice.

MAPLE BACON COOKIE DOUGH

YIELD: SERVES 6 TO 8

What can I say about this maple bacon dough other than . . . bacon! How could it not be good if it has bacon in it? I used imitation maple extract as opposed to real maple extract or maple syrup because I found that when using those other flavoring agents, I couldn't get a strong enough maple flavor. But if you prefer a real maple flavor, use the real extract. Also, if you aren't a bacon fan, just omit it.

1. In a medium skillet, cook the bacon on medium heat until mildly crunchy (feel free to make it more or less crunchy to fit your liking). Once cooked, place it on paper towels to drain and cool. Set aside.

2. In the bowl of a stand mixer fitted with the paddle attachment, cream the butter and sugar together until light and fluffy. It should take about 30 seconds on high. Scrape down the sides of the bowl when done.

3. Add the maple extract and mixed until combined.

4. In a small bowl, whisk together the flour and salt. Gradually add the flour mixture to the butter mixture. Mix on low until fully incorporated.

5. Cut the cooled bacon into small pieces. Fold into the dough by hand until combined.

6. Eat immediately or store in an airtight container for 5 days in the refrigerator or 2 weeks in the freezer.

2 strips of thick-cut maple bacon

1 cup (225 g) butter

½ cup (115 g) lightly packed brown sugar

½ cup (100 g) granulated sugar

½ teaspoon imitation maple extract

1¾ cups (220 g) heat-treated all-purpose flour (page 15)

¼ teaspoon salt

Note:

This dough is amazing to use as a spread on toast or to put a scoop on top of pancakes or waffles for breakfast! If you want to use it as a spread, add 2 to 3 tablespoons (28 to 45 ml) of milk to thin it to your liking.

BUTTER PECAN COOKIE DOUGH

YIELD: SERVES 6 TO 8

If you're a fan of butter pecan, you will fall in love with this recipe. This dough has wonderful caramel and butterscotch flavors that are to die for. The praline candy is very easy to make and gives the dough a true butter pecan flavor. I like to make extra candy and just snack on that while I make the dough. It's that good!

1. To make the praline, first, toast the pecans. It's not a necessary step, but toasting will enhance the pecan's beautiful maple-like flavor. If you don't want to toast your pecans, skip the next step.

2. Place the pecans in a small skillet and heat over medium heat for 3 to 5 minutes. It's easy to burn nuts, so keep a careful eye on them. Stir the nuts frequently to toast them on both sides. You'll know they're done when you can begin to smell them. The second you can smell them, immediately remove them from the heat. They can go from perfect to burnt in a matter of seconds.

3. Let cool briefly and then chop the pecans into bite-size pieces and set aside.

4 In a medium saucepan, melt the butter and the sugars together over medium-high heat. Allow the mixture to boil for 1 minute. Add the evaporated milk and boil for 1 minute longer. Be very careful when you add the evaporated milk because the mixture will boil up vigorously.

5. Remove the mixture from the heat, add the vanilla and reserved pecans, and stir until combined. Carefully pour the hot mixture onto a piece of parchment paper. Spread it out with a spatula and allow it to cool completely until it becomes a soft, sugary solid. It shouldn't take too long to cool, about 15 minutes.

For praline:

½ cup (50 g) pecans

¼ cup (55 g) unsalted butter

¼ cup (60 g) lightly packed brown sugar

¼ cup (50 g) granulated sugar

2 tablespoons (28 ml) evaporated milk

½ teaspoon vanilla extract

For cookie dough:

1 cup (225 g) unsalted butter, softened

1 cup (225 g) lightly packed brown sugar

1 batch of praline (see above)

1 teaspoon vanilla extract

1½ cups (188 g) heat-treated all-purpose flour (page 15)

⅛ teaspoon salt

6. While the praline cools, to make the cookie dough, cream the butter and sugar together in the bowl of a stand mixer fitted with the paddle attachment until light and fluffy. It should take about 30 seconds on high. Scrape down the sides of the bowl when done.

7. Add the cooled soft praline and mix until thoroughly incorporated into the butter. Then, add the vanilla and mix until combined.

8. In a small bowl, whisk together the flour and salt. Gradually add the flour mixture to the butter mixture. Mix on low until the flour is fully incorporated.

9. Eat immediately or store in an airtight container for 2 weeks at room temperature, 1 month in the refrigerator, or 3 months in the freezer.

COOKIE BUTTER COOKIE DOUGH

YIELD: SERVES 6 TO 8

I used to think cookie butter was just cookie dough, so when my good friend and employee Erin suggested a cookie butter flavor, I was quite confused. But as Erin explained to me, cookie butter is a spread made of Biscoff cookies, which are a favorite of both me and my dad. I went to the store and picked myself up a jar, and now I am hooked! This dough is strong in that familiar delicious cookie flavor. Add some crushed Biscoff cookies to bring a wonderful texture to the dough.

1. In the bowl of a stand mixer fitted with the paddle attachment, cream the butter, cookie butter, and sugar together until light and fluffy. It should take about 30 seconds on high. Scrape down the sides of the bowl when done.

2. Add the vanilla and mix until combined.

3. In a small bowl, whisk together the flour and salt. Gradually add the flour mixture to the butter mixture. Mix on low until the flour is fully incorporated.

4. Eat immediately or store in an airtight container for 2 weeks at room temperature, 1 month in the refrigerator, or 3 months in the freezer.

½ cup (112 g) unsalted butter, softened

¾ cup (180 g) cookie butter

¾ cup (150 g) sugar

¼ teaspoon vanilla extract

1¼ cups (156 g) heat-treated all-purpose flour (page 15)

⅛ teaspoon salt

Note:

With this dough, and other doughs where there isn't only butter and sugar in the creaming step, make sure to add the flour slowly. Sometimes these doughs require less flour and can dry out very fast. If you accidentally add too much flour and the dough is dry, add a tablespoon or two (15 to 28 ml) of canola or vegetable oil to rehydrate the dough.

NOT JUST FOR DOGGIES COOKIE DOUGH

YIELD: MAKES ABOUT TWENTY-FOUR 1-TABLESPOON (15 g) SERVINGS

The pups in our life deserve cookie dough, too! They are man's best friend and love us no matter what. Treat them by making this simple and quick dough they are sure to love. It's even a healthy snack for them, so it's a win-win! My service dog, Blu (he's a big black lab), gives it two paws up. Plus, this dough is super delicious to humans!

1. In a large bowl, mash the banana half thoroughly with a fork.

2. Mix in the peanut butter and honey until fully combined.

3. Add the oats and mix until incorporated.

4. Feed your dog about 1 tablespoon (15 g) at a time. Store the rest in the refrigerator for up to 2 weeks.

½ of a large very ripe banana

1 cup (260 g) creamy peanut butter

1 tablespoon (20 g) honey

¾ cup (60 g) quick-cooking oats

Note:

Humans can enjoy this as a protein-packed snack. With just a touch of sweetness and some protein from the peanut butter and oats, it will give you a healthy midday pick-me-up and curb your sweet tooth!

Chapter Two

THINGS TO MAKE
WITH COOKIE DOUGHS

VANILLA CAKE WITH BIRTHDAY CAKE COOKIE DOUGH

YIELD: MAKES ONE 8-INCH (20 CM) LAYER CAKE

I asked a friend of mine who makes beautiful drip-cakes to make me a Birthday Cake Cookie Dough cake for Unbaked's second birthday. It was incredible looking and even better tasting! I wanted to make my own version and again had many trials and errors to create the perfect vanilla cake. Whenever I had tried to bake a vanilla cake previously, it had come out gummy, but this cake has a wonderful soft crumb and rich vanilla flavor. If you want to pair the cake with a different dough, go right ahead. Our Chocolate Cookie Dough would be a great contrast of flavor.

1. Preheat the oven to 350°F (180°C, or gas mark 4). Prepare two 8-inch (20 cm) cake pans by lining them with parchment paper and then spraying them with nonstick cooking spray.

2. Next, prepare a stand mixture fitted with the paddle attachment for the reverse creaming of ingredients. (The reverse creaming method creams the flour and butter together first rather than the sugar and butter to produce a light and moist cake.)

3. In the bowl, mix together the flour, sugar, baking powder, baking soda, and salt. Add the butter to the dry mixture and mix on medium-low speed for 3 minutes. The mixture should resemble very fine crumbs, almost like sand.

4. In a small bowl, whisk together the eggs, sour cream, milk, oil, and vanilla until smooth. Add to the dry mixture all at once, mixing on low until just combined. Do not overmix.

5. Separate the batter evenly between the prepared cake pans. Lightly tap the pans down onto the counter to level the batter and remove any air bubbles.

6. Bake for 35 to 40 minutes until a toothpick inserted into the center of the cakes comes out clean.

3½ cups (438 g) all-purpose flour

1¾ cups (350 g) sugar

1 tablespoon (14 g) baking powder

1 teaspoon baking soda

1 teaspoon salt

½ cup (112 g) unsalted butter, softened

4 eggs

⅔ cup (154 g) sour cream

1⅓ cups (315 ml) milk

½ cup (120 ml) canola oil

1 tablespoon (15 ml) vanilla extract

1 batch of Birthday Cake Cookie Dough (page 23)

Sprinkles or chocolate syrup, for topping (optional)

7. Let the cakes cool for 15 minutes before inverting them out of the pans. Then, allow them to cool completely.

8. Add half of the cookie dough to the top of one of the cakes. Spread the dough with an offset spatula until evenly distributed.

9. Place the second cake on top of the dough. Add the remaining dough to the top of the cake and spread evenly. Add some sprinkles or a chocolate drizzle, if you like, for a fancier-looking cake.

10. Eat immediately or store covered for up to 1 week at room temperature.

Note:
If you want to make this a confetti sprinkle cake, add ¹/₂ cup (60 g) of rainbow sprinkles to the cake batter and fold them in gently by hand until just combined.

PEANUT BUTTER COOKIE DOUGH BROWNIES

YIELD: MAKES 16 BROWNIES

This recipe pairs the classic duo of peanut butter and chocolate in an unbelievably delicious and fudgy brownie. This old-fashioned brownie recipe is adapted from my Grandma Gloria's recipe. She told me I wasn't allowed to use the exact recipe (she's keen on keeping family secrets), so I promised I'd change it up a bit. This version tastes even better, but don't tell her that!

1. Preheat the oven to 350°F (180°C, or gas mark 4). Spray an 8-inch (20 cm) square pan with nonstick cooking spray.

2. In a large bowl, cream the butter and sugar together until light and fluffy. Add the eggs one at a time. Add the chocolate syrup and mix.

3. Add the flour and salt all at once to the wet mixture. Do not overmix.

4. Add the vanilla and mix until just combined. Set the batter aside.

5. Drop 16 tablespoon-size (15 g) balls of Peanut Butter Cookie Dough into the bottom of the pan. Set the remaining dough aside.

6. Pour the batter into the pan and spread it evenly over the dough balls with a spatula. Lightly tap the pan down onto the counter to level the batter and remove any air bubbles.

7. Bake for 55 to 60 minutes until the center no longer jiggles if the pan is jostled. The top of the brownies will still look like wet batter. That's okay—they are fully baked, I promise. Allow the brownies to cool completely.

8. Add the oil, if using, to the remaining Peanut Butter Cookie Dough. This will allow the dough to have more of a frosting texture, but you can skip it if you prefer.

9. Spread the dough "frosting" on the top of the brownies. Add toppings such as sprinkles or mini peanut butter cups, if you'd like.

10. Eat immediately or cover and store for up to one week at room temperature.

½ cup (112 g) unsalted butter, softened

1 cup (200 g) sugar

2 eggs

1½ cups (355 ml) chocolate syrup

1 cup plus 1 tablespoon (133 g) all-purpose flour

¼ teaspoon salt

1 teaspoon vanilla extract

1 batch of Peanut Butter Cookie Dough (see page 71)

1 tablespoon (15 ml) vegetable oil (optional)

Sprinkles or mini peanut butter cups, for topping (optional)

Note:

If you prefer a more cake-like brownie, add 1 additional egg. If you are allergic to peanut butter or just aren't a fan, feel free to swap the dough for any other flavor.

CHOCOLATE CHIP CAKE WITH CHOCOLATE CHIP COOKIE DOUGH FILLING

YIELD: MAKES ONE 8-INCH (20 CM) LAYER CAKE

When thinking of layer cake flavors to create, I wanted a cake with Chocolate Chip Cookie Dough filling. I was going to pair it with a chocolate cake, but then I thought an actual chocolate chip cake would be amazing. I made it my mission to try to create a chocolate chip cake, and after several tries, I think I created a winner. This cake is piled with chocolate chip flavor!

1. Preheat the oven to 350°F (180°C, or gas mark 4). Prepare two 8-inch (20 cm) cake pans by lining them with parchment paper and then spraying them with nonstick cooking spray.

2. Next, prepare a stand mixture fitted with the paddle attachment for the reverse creaming of ingredients. (The reverse creaming method creams the flour and butter together first rather than the sugar and butter to produce a light and moist cake.)

3. In the bowl, mix together 3½ cups (438 g) of the flour, the sugars, baking powder, baking soda, and salt. Add the butter to the dry mixture and mix on medium-low speed for about 2 minutes. The mixture should resemble very fine crumbs, almost like sand.

4. In a small bowl, whisk together the eggs, milk, oil, and vanilla. Add them to the dry mixture all at once, mixing on low until just combined. Do not overmix or the cake will become dense.

3½ cups (438 g) all-purpose flour plus 2 tablespoons (16 g) for chocolate chips

1 cup (200 g) granulated sugar

1 cup (225 g) lightly packed brown sugar

2½ teaspoons (12 g) baking powder

1 teaspoon baking soda

1 teaspoon salt

½ cup (112 g) unsalted butter, softened

4 eggs

1 cup (235 ml) milk

⅔ cup (160 ml) canola oil

1 teaspoon vanilla extract

1 cup (175 g) mini semisweet chocolate chips, plus more for topping (optional)

1 batch of Chocolate Chip Cookie Dough (page 72)

Chocolate syrup, for topping (optional)

5. In another small bowl, place the chocolate chips. Add the remaining 2 tablespoons (28 g) of flour and mix to evenly coat the chips. This will keep the chips from sinking to the bottom of the pans when baking. Add the chips to the batter and fold in by hand until just combined.

6. Separate the batter evenly between the prepared cake pans. Lightly tap the pans down onto the counter to level the batter and remove any air bubbles.

7. Bake for 35 to 40 minutes until a toothpick inserted into the center of the cakes comes out clean.

8. Let the cakes cool for 15 minutes before inverting them out of the pans. Then, allow them to cool completely.

9. Add half of the cookie dough to the top of one of the cakes. Spread the dough with an offset spatula until evenly distributed.

10. Place the second cake on top of the dough. Add the remaining dough to the top of the cake and spread evenly. Add more chocolate chips to the top or a chocolate drizzle, if you like, to create a fancier-looking cake.

11. Eat immediately or store covered for up to 1 week at room temperature.

CHOCOLATE CHIP COOKIE DOUGH CHEESECAKE

YIELD: MAKES ONE 10-INCH (25.5 CM) CHEESECAKE

I'm a sucker for cheesecake, so I knew I had to incorporate cookie dough into a cheesecake recipe. I've chosen to use Chocolate Chip Cookie Dough, but feel free to use any flavor of dough you'd like.

1. Preheat the oven to 325°F (170°C, or gas mark 3).

2. In a large bowl, cream the cream cheese and sugar together with a handheld mixer until smooth and fluffy, about 1 minute. Scrape down the sides of the bowl and add the eggs one at a time, mixing well after each addition. Mix in the vanilla.

3. Place teaspoon-size balls of Chocolate Chip Cookie Dough around the bottom of the piecrust. I fit in 19 dough balls. If you want more dough in there, add more. If you want less, feel free to add less.

4. Pour the cheesecake mixture over the crust and dough balls. Carefully spread out the cheesecake mixture with a spatula to evenly cover the dough balls and fill the crust.

5. Bake for 40 to 45 minutes until the center of the cheesecake is almost set. It should still jiggle in the middle if gently shaken.

6. Let the cheesecake cool for 1 hour in the refrigerator. When it's cool to the touch, use an ice cream scoop to arrange the remaining dough on top of the cheesecake.

7. Fill a plastic bag (or piping bag) with the chocolate syrup. Snip off a small corner of the plastic bag, just big enough to drizzle the syrup on top of the cheesecake. Gently squeeze the syrup over the dough and cheesecake, using quick stokes to form a decorative drizzle.

8. Place the cheesecake in the refrigerator and let chill for at least 3 hours before serving.

9. Eat immediately or store covered for up to 1 week in the refrigerator or tightly wrapped in the freezer for up to 2 months.

2 packages (8 ounces, or 225 g each) of cream cheese, softened

½ cup (100 g) sugar

2 eggs

¾ teaspoon vanilla extract

1 batch of Chocolate Chip Cookie Dough (page 18)

1 graham cracker piecrust (10 inches, or 25.5 cm)

½ cup (120 ml) chocolate syrup (see page 78, or use store-bought)

CHOCOLATE CHIP COOKIE DOUGH SANDWICHES

YIELD: MAKES 18 SANDWICHES

This chocolate chip cookie recipe is one of the best you'll ever try, I promise. These cookies hold their shape and turn into scrumptious thick cookies. I personally love thick cookies, but if you prefer a flat and crunchy cookie, feel free to substitute your favorite cookie recipe, whether it's chocolate chip or another flavor entirely, to create the cookie part of your sandwiches. You really can mix and match with any cookie and cookie dough flavor to create your perfect cookie dough sammie!

3⅔ cups (458 g) all-purpose flour

2¾ teaspoons (13 g) baking powder

1 teaspoon salt

1¼ cups (280 g) unsalted butter, softened

1¼ cups (285 g) lightly packed brown sugar

1 cup (200 g) granulated sugar

2 eggs

2 teaspoons vanilla extract

2 cups (350 g) semisweet chocolate chips

1 batch of edible cookie dough of choice

½ cup (weight will vary) topping of choice (Make sure the texture is small enough to coat the edges of the cookies.)

1. Preheat the oven to 375°F (190°C, or gas mark 5). Line a baking sheet with parchment paper.

2. In a small bowl, combine the flour, baking powder, and salt.

3. In the bowl of a stand mixer fitted with the paddle attachment, cream together the butter and the sugars. Whip on high speed for about 1 minute until the mixture turns light and fluffy. Scrape down the sides of the bowl.

4. Add the eggs one at a time, mixing well after each. Then, mix in the vanilla.

5. Gradually add the flour mixture to the butter mixture and mix until just combined. Don't overmix the dough or your cookies will be tough. Fold in the chocolate chips by hand.

6. Using an ice cream scoop, scoop about 1½ tablespoons (23 g) of the dough onto the prepared baking sheet, spacing them about 2 inches (5 cm) apart.

7. Bake for 13 to 16 minutes until the cookies are golden brown on the edges.

8. Using a spatula, carefully transfer the cookies to a cooling rack. Allow them to cool completely.

9. Add a small scoop of edible cookie dough to the bottom of a cookie. Add another cookie to the top and gently squish the cookies together until the dough comes to the edges of the cookies. Gently roll the cookie sandwich edges in the topping of your choice. Repeat with the remaining cookies and dough.

10. Eat immediately or store covered for up to 1 week at room temperature.

Note:
To make an extra-impressive cookie sammie, dip one half of each sandwich in melted chocolate. Yum!

EDIBLE COOKIE DOUGH TRUFFLES

YIELD: MAKES ABOUT 36 TRUFFLES

These cute truffles have a luscious center and a crunchy exterior. You can eat them on the go, pop them for a snack, and if you feel like sharing, you could even bring them to a party. These truffles also make a lovely gift when placed in a cute gift box.

> 1 batch of edible cookie dough of choice
>
> 2 cups (350 g) chocolate chips of choice
>
> 3 tablespoons (45 ml) vegetable oil
>
> ½ cup (weight will vary) topping of choice

1. Line a baking sheet with parchment paper. Measure out tablespoon-size (15 g) scoops of the cookie dough, roll them into a ball, and then place them onto the baking sheet. I use a small ice cream scoop for uniform balls, but a spoon will work just fine.

2. Place the balls in the freezer for at least 30 minutes while you prepare the coating. This will allow them to firm up and make them easy to dip in the chocolate.

3. In a microwave-safe bowl, place the chocolate chips. Place the bowl in the microwave and cook on high in 20-second intervals. After each interval, stir the chips. Don't worry if the chips aren't melted after the first one or two intervals. We are faux-tempering the chocolate by doing this and keeping it from burning.

4. Once the chocolate is fully melted, add the oil. Fully mix it into the chocolate to create a thinner chocolate that's very shiny.

5. Take the truffles out of the freezer and set up a little assembly line to dip and coat them with the topping. There are a few ways you can dip your truffles. You can place them on top of a fork and dip them that way. You can also use a toothpick to skewer them, which is a method I came up with that saved the day for me. (I used to be terrible at making truffles until I did it this way!)

6. If you'd like to use the toothpick method, take a toothpick and dip just the end into the melted chocolate. Then, insert the toothpick into the center of the cookie dough ball. Repeat for the remaining balls and then place the cookie sheet back into the freezer for 30 seconds.

7. The cookie dough balls are ready to be fully coated. Pick up one of the balls by the toothpick and gently dip it into the chocolate. Coat the entire ball and then allow the excess to drip off back into the bowl. Scrape the bottom of the truffle on the side of the bowl and then place it back down on the parchment paper.

8. Allow the chocolate to harden slightly (maybe 10 seconds) and then carefully twirl the toothpick free. There will be a little hole, but don't worry—the topping will cover it up!

9. Working quickly once you get the toothpick out, sprinkle the ball with your topping of choice. Make sure you do this before the chocolate fully sets or your topping won't stick. Repeat for the remaining balls. Allow the chocolate to completely harden before eating. You can place them into the refrigerator to speed up this process.

10. Eat immediately or store in an airtight container for 2 weeks at room temperature or 1 month in the refrigerator. These also freeze well in an airtight container for 2 months.

STUFFED CHOCOLATE SANDWICH COOKIES

YIELD: MAKES 40 SANDWICH COOKIES

This recipe features a special dough that incorporates the filling of the sandwich cookies into the dough. The filling is totally the best part of the sandwich cookie, and this recipe makes that the star! You absolutely don't have to use this dough flavor, though. You can use any dough for the inside of the sandwich cookies. To finish them, they're dipped in chocolate, but if you'd rather just have the cookie alone, skip the dipping steps.

1. Line a baking sheet with parchment paper.

2. Carefully separate the sandwich cookies and gently scrape the filling into the bowl of a stand mixer. Set the cookies off to the side and reserve.

3. To make the cookie dough, add the butter to the bowl of cookie filling and mix on low until fully incorporated. Add the sugar to the butter mixture and cream together for about 1 minute on high until light and fluffy. Scrape down the sides of the bowl when done.

4. Add the vanilla and mix until combined.

5. In a small bowl, whisk together the flour and salt. Gradually add the flour mixture to the butter mixture until fully incorporated.

6. Place about a tablespoon-size (15 g) spoonful of cookie dough onto a reserved cookie half. Press another cookie half on top of the dough and gently press until the dough reaches the sides of the cookies. Place it on the baking sheet and repeat for the remaining cookies. Place them in the freezer for at least 30 minutes.

7. In a microwave safe bowl, place the chocolate chips. Place the bowl in the microwave and cook on high in 20-second intervals. After each interval, stir the chips. Don't worry if the chips aren't melted after the first one or two

40 chocolate sandwich cookies

1 cup (225 g) unsalted butter, softened

⅔ cup (133 g) sugar

¼ teaspoon vanilla extract

1¾ cups (220 g) heat-treated all-purpose flour (page 15)

⅛ teaspoon salt

2 cups (350 g) chocolate chips of choice

2 teaspoons vegetable oil

1 cup (weight will vary) topping of choice (make sure the pieces aren't too big)

intervals. We are faux-tempering the chocolate. Once the chocolate is fully melted, add the oil. Fully mix it into the chocolate to create a thinner chocolate for coating.

8. Take the cookie sandwiches out of the freezer and set up a little assembly line to dip and coat them with the topping. There are a few ways you can dip the cookies. You can place them on top of a fork and dip them that way. You can also use a toothpick.

9. If you'd like to use the toothpick method, take a toothpick and dip just the end into the chocolate coating. Then, insert the toothpick into the center of the cookie dough part of the cookie sandwich. Repeat for the remaining sandwiches and then place the baking sheet back into the freezer for 30 seconds.

10. The cookies are ready to be fully coated. Pick up one of the cookies by the toothpick and gently dip it into the chocolate. Coat the entire surface and then allow the excess to drip off back into the bowl before placing it back down on the parchment paper.

11. Working quickly, sprinkle the cookie sandwich with the topping. Make sure you do this before the chocolate fully sets or your topping won't stick. Repeat for the remaining cookies and then place them back into the freezer to allow the chocolate to set up, about 5 minutes. Carefully remove the toothpick from the side of the cookie before serving.

12. Eat immediately or store covered for 1 week at room temperature, 1 month in the refrigerator, or 3 months in the freezer.

COOKIE DOUGH–STUFFED ICE CREAM CONES

YIELD: MAKES 15 CONES

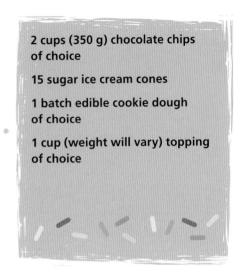

2 cups (350 g) chocolate chips of choice

15 sugar ice cream cones

1 batch edible cookie dough of choice

1 cup (weight will vary) topping of choice

These stuffed ice cream cones are unbelievably cute and the perfect treat to serve at a birthday party. Forget about cupcakes: These are the new go-to goodie to serve. They store incredibly well since the dough is sealed into the cone by the chocolate. Get the kiddos to help you make these. They'll have a blast dipping the cones into the chocolate and the toppings!

1. Line a baking sheet with parchment paper.

2. Place the chocolate chips in a microwave-safe bowl and cook in the microwave on high for 20-second intervals. Stir after each interval and continue until all of the chips are completely melted.

3. Pour about 1 tablespoon (15 ml) of melted chocolate into the bottom of each cone.

4. Carefully stuff about 2 tablespoons (28 g) of cookie dough into each cone. Press lightly on the dough to make sure it gets as deep into the cone as possible, but don't press so hard that you crack your cone. Level off the top of each cone and then place it upside down on the baking sheet.

5. Place the stuffed cones in the freezer and allow them to harden for at least 30 minutes.

6. While the cones cool, set up an assembly line with your remaining melted chocolate and topping/toppings. You may need to rewarm the chocolate before you start dipping.

7. When ready to dip the cones, dip the open end (wide end) of a cone into the melted chocolate. You can dip as far as you want. I dipped mine until there was about 1 inch (2.5 cm) of chocolate on the side of the cone. Allow some of the excess chocolate to drip off the cone back into the bowl and then dip the into the topping. You can simply dip the top or roll the edges to allow the topping to get on the sides of the cone as well. Place the cone back down onto the baking sheet. They won't stick, so don't worry about placing them down on the melted chocolate.

8. Repeat for the remaining cones and then place the cones back in the freezer to allow them to fully set, about 15 minutes. Allow the cones to come to room temperature before serving.

9. Store the cones for 2 weeks at room temperature, 1 month in the refrigerator, or 3 months in the freezer.

HOMEMADE COOKIE DOUGH ICE CREAM

YIELD: SERVES 6 TO 8

Cookie dough ice cream is one of the most popular ice cream flavors in America, and this homemade version is even better than the store-bought stuff. Homemade ice cream is so delicious, and it's actually pretty easy to make, so don't shy away from this recipe. This ice cream base recipe is for a super-creamy and luscious vanilla bean flavor, but feel free to use whatever ice cream base flavor and recipe you'd like. This base recipe is a great blank canvas to add other flavoring agents to as well, such as mint extract or macerated strawberries.

1. In a medium saucepan, heat the cream and half-and-half on low heat.

2. Slice the vanilla bean down the middle (don't cut it all of the way through) and place it in the cream mixture. Allow the cream and vanilla bean to steep together for 10 minutes. Stir pretty often so that a film doesn't develop. The mixture should never begin to simmer or boil; you just want to warm it up.

3. While the cream steeps, in a small bowl, whisk together the egg yolks and sugar. It will be a very thick paste, and that's okay.

4. After 10 minutes, remove the vanilla bean from the cream. Add ½ cup (120 ml) of the hot cream to the egg mixture, whisking continuously and vigorously while you do. This will temper the eggs so that they can be heated further without becoming scrambled eggs. If you don't whisk the eggs while adding the hot cream, the eggs will scramble then, too. So don't forget!

5. After you've tempered the eggs, place the mixture in the saucepan and heat it on medium-low heat for about 5 minutes or until the mixture thickens slightly. You'll know it's ready when the mixture coats the back of a spoon and you can draw a line down the middle with your finger.

2 cups (475 ml) heavy cream

1 cup (235 ml) half-and-half

1 vanilla bean

4 egg yolks

1 cup (200 g) sugar

2 teaspoons vanilla bean paste

Pinch of salt

½ of a batch of edible cookie dough of choice

6. Remove the mixture from the heat, add the vanilla bean paste and salt, and whisk until combined.

7. Strain the mixture into a large bowl and cover with plastic wrap. When you cover it with the plastic wrap, set the wrap directly down onto the surface of the mixture. This will prevent a film from forming. Place the mixture in the refrigerator and allow it to cool for at least 3 hours.

8. When the mixture is ready, churn it in an ice cream maker according to the manufacturer's instructions.

9. When the ice cream is ready, transfer it to a large bowl and fold in teaspoon-size chunks or balls of the edible cookie dough by hand.

10. Eat the ice cream immediately as soft serve or place it in an airtight container and freeze for at least 3 hours for regular ice cream. Store the ice cream for up to 1 month in the freezer.

Note:

If you don't have vanilla beans or vanilla bean paste, don't worry. You can still make this delicious ice cream! Just use 1 tablespoon (15 ml) of vanilla extract in place of the bean and paste.

COOKIE DOUGH PIE

YIELD: MAKES ONE 8- OR 9-INCH (20 OR 23 CM) PIE

This cookie dough pie is everything you'd want it to be—plus more, with its secret layer of gooey white chocolate ganache. Make this pie with any cookie dough and topping combination you'd like. Add a chocolate drizzle on top and whipped cream when serving to add even more texture and richness. If you don't have time to make a crust, use a store-bought one for a just-as-amazing result.

1. Preheat the oven to 350°F (180°C, or gas mark 4).

2. In a food processor or blender, blend the cookies into fine crumbs. You can also do this by hand if you'd like. Just place your cookies into a large resealable plastic bag and seal it with nearly all of the air out of it. Using a rolling pin or another heavy kitchen utensil, smash the bag to break up the cookies. Try to get them as fine as you can. The crumbs need to be fine or the crust won't form correctly.

24 chocolate sandwich cookies

5 tablespoons (70 g) unsalted butter, melted

¾ cup (131 g) semisweet chocolate chips

2 tablespoons (28 ml) heavy cream

1 batch edible cookie dough of choice

½ cup (weight will vary) topping of choice

3. Place the crumbs into a bowl with the melted butter. Stir together until the butter has coated all of the crumbs.

4. Pour the crumbs into an 8- or 9-inch (20 or 23 cm) springform pan. Firmly press the crumbs down evenly over the bottom of the pan.

5. Bake the crust for 10 minutes. When done, place it into the refrigerator for 30 minutes to cool and set.

6. Place the chocolate chips and heavy cream in a small microwave-safe bowl. Microwave the chocolate and cream on high for 30 seconds. Stir the chocolate and cream together until a smooth, thick ganache forms. If the chocolate chips haven't all melted, heat it in 15-second intervals until all of the chips have melted.

7. When the crust is completely cool (it doesn't have to be cold, but make sure it's cool), spread the ganache evenly over it. Place it back into the refrigerator for 15 minutes to allow the ganache to firm up.

8. Add the dough to the pan and spread it evenly over the ganache. Sprinkle the topping over the top of the cookie dough. Place the pie in the refrigerator and allow it to chill for 1 hour.

9. When ready to serve, run a knife around the side of the pan. Undo and remove the side of the springform pan. It's easier to cut the pie when it's slightly cold, but its best eaten closer to room temperature.

10. Eat immediately or store covered for up to 1 week in the refrigerator. Freeze the pie in an airtight container or wrapped tightly in plastic wrap for up to 3 months.

Note:

If you want to use a cookie dough that doesn't go with a chocolate sandwich cookie crust or chocolate ganache, swap it for a graham cracker crust and white chocolate ganache. Below are the recipes for each. Follow the instructions for their chocolate counterparts when making them.

For graham cracker crust:

1½ cups (126 g) fine graham cracker crumbs

5 tablespoons (70 g) unsalted butter, melted

For white chocolate ganache:

¾ cup (168 g) white chocolate chips

2 tablespoons (28 ml) heavy cream

Note:

You can also add a glaze to the top of the pie, if you like. In a medium bowl, melt ½ cup (120 ml) of heavy cream and 1½ cups (336 g) of white chocolate chips in the microwave on high in 30-second intervals. Stir until a smooth glaze forms. Allow it to cool completely before pouring it over the pie.

COOKIE DOUGH–STUFFED CUPCAKES

YIELD: MAKES 18 CUPCAKES

I know I said earlier that cupcakes were old news compared to cookie dough–stuffed ice cream cones, but these cookie dough–stuffed cupcakes still make the cut. It's an easy cupcake and frosting recipe that you can whip up in a matter of minutes. The cupcakes are very fluffy and moist, and the frosting is creamy and not overly sweet. Decorate your cupcakes however you want, such as topping them with sprinkles or drizzling them with chocolate syrup.

1. Preheat the oven to 350°F (180°C, or gas mark 4). Line two cupcake pans with cupcake liners.

2. In a large bowl, mix together the cake mix, milk, oil, and sour cream until combined.

3. Add the eggs and vanilla all at once and mix until smooth, about 30 seconds.

4. Fill the cupcake liners two-thirds of the way full. Don't go over two-thirds full or your cupcakes will overflow and won't have a nice domed shape.

5. Bake the cupcakes for 15 to 17 minutes until just baked through. You don't want them to be brown at all. Mine took 16 minutes. You'll know they're done when the cake bounces back when you touch it or a toothpick inserted into the middle comes out clean.

6. Allow the cupcakes to cool completely on a wire rack.

CONTINUED ON NEXT PAGE

For cupcakes:

3 cups (375 g) boxed cake mix of your choice (about 1 full box)

½ cup (120 ml) milk

½ cup (120 ml) vegetable oil

½ cup (115 g) sour cream

3 eggs

1 teaspoon vanilla extract

1 batch of edible cookie dough of choice

Sprinkles or other topping of choice (optional)

7. To make the frosting, whip the butter and cream cheese together in a bowl of a stand mixer fitted with the whisk attachment until smooth and very white in color.

8. Add the confectioners' sugar a little at a time and mix until combined. Then, turn your mixer to high and whip for about 30 seconds.

9. Add the vanilla and salt and mix until combined. Set the frosting aside.

10. When the cupcakes are cool, with your finger, squash the middle of each cupcake down until your finger hits the bottom of the wrapper. You can use a cupcake or apple corer for this step, but why waste cake? Place the edible cookie dough into a large plastic bag with a corner cut off or a piping bag. Carefully fill each cupcake's hole with the dough. Make sure you completely fill the hole so there are no gaps when you bite into the cupcake.

11. Place the frosting into another piping bag and pipe it onto the cupcakes. You can be fancy or simple with your frosting design, whatever you prefer. Top the cupcakes with sprinkles or another topping of your choice, if you'd like.

12. Eat immediately or store covered for about 1 week at room temperature.

For the frosting:

½ cup (112 g) unsalted butter, softened

8 ounces (225 g) cream cheese

4 cups (480 g) powdered sugar

1 teaspoon vanilla extract

Pinch of salt

DEVIL'S FOOD CAKE WITH PEANUT BUTTER COOKIE DOUGH

YIELD: MAKES ONE 9-INCH (23 CM) LAYER CAKE

This is my all-time favorite cake recipe because it is so easy! It tastes pretty darn good, too. All you need is one big bowl and a sturdy spoon. In the instructions I say to use a stand mixer, but feel free to just mix this by hand (which I often do). It's very simple to make and gives you a light, airy cake that packs a chocolate punch. If you aren't a coffee fan, don't be alarmed. You won't taste the coffee in the recipe. It is used simply to enhance the chocolate flavor.

2 cups (250 g) all-purpose flour

2 cups (400 g) sugar

¾ cup (60 g) unsweetened cocoa powder

1 teaspoon baking powder

2 teaspoons baking soda

½ teaspoon salt

1 cup (235 ml) milk

1 cup (235 ml) vegetable oil

¾ cup (175 ml) freshly brewed coffee

2 eggs

1 teaspoon vanilla extract

1 batch of Peanut Butter Cookie Dough (see page 71)

Mini peanut butter cups or chocolate syrup, for topping (optional)

1. Preheat the oven to 325°F (170°C, or gas mark 3). Prepare two 9-inch (23 cm) cake pans by lining them with parchment paper and then spraying them with nonstick cooking spray.

2. In the bowl of a stand mixer fitted with the paddle attachment, mix together the flour, sugar, cocoa powder, baking powder, baking soda, and salt.

3. Add the milk, oil, and coffee all at once and mix. Add the eggs and vanilla and mix for about 1 minute. The batter should be shiny and somewhat thin.

4. Separate the batter evenly between the prepared cake pans. Lightly tap the pans down onto the counter to level the batter and remove any air bubbles.

5. Bake for 50 minutes or until a toothpick inserted into the center of the cakes comes out clean.

6. Let the cakes cool for 15 minutes before inverting them out of the pans. Then, allow them to cool completely.

7. Evenly spread half of the Peanut Butter Cookie Dough on the top of one of the cakes.

8. Place the second cake on top of the dough. Add the remaining dough to the top of the cake and spread evenly. Add some mini peanut butter cups or a chocolate drizzle, if you like, for a fancier-looking cake.

9. Eat immediately or cover and store for up to one week at room temperature.

PEANUT BUTTER COOKIE DOUGH CANDY BARS

YIELD: MAKES 18 CANDY BARS

Boy oh boy, is this recipe fantastic! It was by far my family and friend's favorite recipe I tested out while creating this book. It is everything you want in a candy bar. There's caramel, chocolate, and peanut butter. What's not to love? The sugar wafers add an amazing crunch to the smooth and creamy caramel and peanut butter. Bring these bars to any party and your friends will be begging for the recipe.

1. First, get out an 8-inch (20 cm) square pan that is at least 2 inches (5 cm) high. Cut a piece of parchment paper that is the width of the pan and long enough to go up and over the sides of the pan. Cut another piece of the same size to go in the other direction. You'll end up with the entire pan lined with parchment paper and four flaps on either side.

2. Place 1½ cups (263 g) of the chocolate chips in a microwave-safe bowl and heat on high in 20-second intervals. Stir after each interval and continue until all of the chips are completely melted.

3. Pour the melted chocolate over the bottom of the prepared pan. Spread the chocolate evenly over the bottom and up the sides of the pan. You can use a small spatula or even a pastry brush to completely spread the chocolate. Once the entire bottom and sides are covered, place in the refrigerator for 20 minutes.

4. Place the unwrapped caramel candies and water in a microwave-safe bowl and heat on high until fully melted, about 1 to 2 minutes. Stir after each minute. Allow to cool slightly, but not enough for it to harden back up.

5. Pour the caramel over the chocolate-covered pan and quickly spread it over just the bottom of the pan. The chocolate may begin to melt if it's not cold enough or if the caramel is too warm. That's okay. Just do your best to get the caramel spread over the bottom. Place in the refrigerator for 10 minutes.

3 cups (525 g) milk chocolate chips

8 ounces (225 g) soft caramel candies (about 25 of the individually wrapped squares)

2 tablespoons (28 ml) water

1 batch of Peanut Butter Cookie Dough (page 71)

28 vanilla sugar wafers

6. After the caramel has cooled, spread half of the Peanut Butter Cookie Dough evenly over the bottom of the pan. Use a spare piece of parchment paper to push the dough down to ensure there are no air pockets.

7. Place half of the vanilla sugar wafers over the dough, pressing them in slightly. I fit 14 wafers in two rows perfectly. If your count needs adjusting, do what you need to make the wafers fit. Repeat the layers, spreading the rest of the dough and wafers in the pan. Refrigerate for 10 minutes.

8. Melt the remaining 1½ cups (263 g) of chocolate chips in the microwave, again in 20-second intervals. Pour over the top of the wafers and spread evenly to completely cover them. The chocolate should completely seal the top. Refrigerate for 1 hour until everything is very set.

9. Once it's been chilled, flip the pan over onto a cutting board. It should slide right out because of the parchment layer on the bottom of the pan. If it doesn't, run a knife between the pan and the parchment to loosen any chocolate that may have seeped under the parchment. Cut into candy bar-size or bite-size pieces.

10. Eat immediately or store covered for 2 weeks at room temperature, 1 month in the refrigerator, or 3 months in the freezer.

COOKIE DOUGH PARTY DIP

YIELD: SERVES 6 TO 8

You know the party has started when the cookie dough dip is served! Make a dip out of any of the cookie doughs in this book by simply adding milk to thin the dough out. Have fun when making your dip. You can do almost anything to it. Stir toppings into the dough or sprinkle them on top. Add some whipped cream. It's all up to you. As to what you should dip into the dough, that's completely up to you, too. I've provided a list of some popular (and some of my favorite) dipping items to give you some ideas.

1. In a large bowl, mix the cookie dough and 2 tablespoons (28 ml) of the milk together with a handheld mixer until smooth and creamy. If the dough seems too thick, add 1 tablespoon (15 ml) more of milk at a time until it reaches your desired consistency.

2. Place the dip in a bowl and drizzle with the chocolate or (and) caramel sauces. Add a topping to the top, too, if you'd like!

3. Place the bowl onto a large plate and arrange the dipping items around the bowl.

4. Get to dippin' and eat immediately or store in an airtight container for 3 weeks in the refrigerator or 2 months in the freezer.

1 batch of edible cookie dough of choice

2 to 4 tablespoons (28 to 60 ml) milk

¼ cup (60 ml) chocolate or caramel sauce

For dipping:

Graham crackers

Pretzels

Marshmallows

Cookies

Brownies

Pound cake

Puffed rice cereal treats

Strawberries

SNICKERDOODLE COOKIE DOUGH COFFEE CAKE

YIELD: MAKES ONE 8-INCH (20 CM) CAKE

This cake is one of my favorite breakfast treats to make. It's moist and has a wonderful light crumb. The streusel topping is full of cinnamon and brown sugar flavor, and then to top that all off (literally), Snickerdoodle Cookie Dough is added. Yum! It's a super-easy cake that is well worth the time. Feel free to top this cake with any kind of cookie dough you'd like. Coffee Cookie Dough (page 76) or Oatmeal Cookie Dough (page 66) would be a great alternative.

2 cups (250 g) all-purpose flour

1 cup (200 g) sugar

½ cup plus 2 tablespoons (140 g) unsalted butter, cold

1 teaspoon baking soda

½ teaspoon baking powder

½ teaspoon salt

⅔ cup (160 ml) milk

2 tablespoons (28 g) sour cream

1 egg

1 teaspoon vanilla bean paste

⅔ cup (150 g) lightly packed brown sugar

2 teaspoons ground cinnamon

1 batch of Snickerdoodle Cookie Dough (page 67)

1. Preheat the oven to 350°F (180°C, or gas mark 4). Prepare an 8-inch (20 cm) springform pan by spraying it liberally with nonstick cooking spray.

2. In a large bowl, whisk the flour and sugar briefly to combine.

3. Cut the cold butter into chunks and add them to the flour mixture. Using a pastry blender or fork, cut the cold butter chunks into the flour and sugar. It should have a sand-like texture with large butter chunks.

4. Measure out 1 cup (125 g) of the flour mixture, place it in a small bowl, and reserve. You will use this to create the streusel topping.

5. Going back to the main flour mixture, add the baking soda, baking powder, and salt and whisk until combined.

6. Add the milk, sour cream, and egg and with a handheld mixer, mix together until a smooth batter forms. The batter will be very thick, but that's how it's supposed to be. Add the vanilla bean paste and mix.

7. Spoon the batter into the prepared pan, spreading it evenly.

8. Going back to the reserved flour mixture, add the brown sugar and cinnamon and mix together until the brown sugar and cinnamon are evenly distributed throughout the mixture. Add the streusel topping to the prepared pan and gently spread it evenly over the top of the batter.

9. Bake for 45 to 50 minutes until a toothpick inserted into the middle of the cake comes out clean.

10. Allow the cake to cool for 30 minutes. Once it's somewhat cool, add teaspoon-size chunks of the Snickerdoodle Cookie Dough to the top of the cake.

11. Eat the cake warm or allow to cool completely before covering and storing for up to 1 week at room temperature.

COOKIE DOUGH PRETZEL BITES

YIELD: MAKES ABOUT 36 PRETZEL BITES

This recipe is basically a sweet-and-salty version of the Edible Cookie Dough Truffles on page 114. The pretzels add a fantastic crunch and salty contrast to the creamy, sweet dough. Use any dough for this recipe. I highly recommend the Peanut Butter Cookie Dough (page 71)!

1 batch of edible cookie dough of choice

36 mini pretzel twists

2 cups (350 g) chocolate chips of choice

3 tablespoons (45 ml) vegetable oil

½ cup (weight will vary) topping of choice

1. Line a baking sheet with parchment paper. Measure out 36 teaspoon-size scoops of your cookie dough and roll them into balls.

2. Place a ball of dough onto a pretzel twist. Place another pretzel twist on top and gently squash the dough ball between the pretzels. Then, place it onto the baking sheet. Repeat with the remaining pretzels and dough balls. Place the baking sheet in the freezer for at least 30 minutes.

3. In a microwave-safe bowl, place the chocolate chips. Heat in the microwave on high in 20-second intervals. After each interval, stir the chips. Don't worry if the chips aren't melted after the first one or two intervals. Once the chocolate is fully melted, add the oil. Fully mix it into the chocolate to create a thinner chocolate for coating our pretzel bites.

4. Take the pretzel bites out of the freezer and set up a little assembly line to dip and coat them with your toppings. There are a few ways you can dip them. You can place them on top of a fork and dip them that way. You can also use a toothpick.

5. If you'd like to use the toothpick method, take a toothpick and dip just the end into the chocolate coating. Then, insert the toothpick into the center of the cookie dough part of the prezel bite. Repeat for the remaining pretzel bites and then place the cookie sheet back into the freezer for 30 seconds.

6. Now, the pretzel bites are ready to be coated. Pick up one of the pretzels by the toothpick and gently dip it into the chocolate. Coat the entire pretzel bite and then allow the excess to drip off back into the bowl. Place it back down onto the parchment paper.

7. Allow the chocolate to harden slightly (maybe 10 seconds) and then carefully twirl the toothpick free. There will be a little hole, but don't worry—the toppings will cover it up!

8. Working quickly once you get the toothpick out, sprinkle the pretzel bite with the topping. Make sure you do this before the chocolate fully sets or your topping won't stick. Repeat for the remaining pretzel bites.

9. Allow the chocolate to completely harden before eating. You can place them in the refrigerator to speed up this process. Eat immediately or store in an airtight container for 2 weeks at room temperature, 1 month in the refrigerator, or 3 months in the freezer.

COOKIE DOUGH ICE CREAM SANDWICHES

YIELD: MAKES 12 SANDWICHES

These ice cream sandwiches are anything but average. They're like eating cookie dough ice cream on steroids. Instead of using cookies as the sandwich part, we will be using cookie dough. You may be confused as to how exactly cookie dough can be used as the sandwich part, but don't worry, I'll walk you through exactly what to do. You can roll the sides of your sandwiches in toppings or even dip one side of them into melted chocolate for an even more impressive sammie!

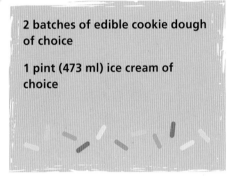

2 batches of edible cookie dough of choice

1 pint (473 ml) ice cream of choice

1. Line two 9 x 13-inch (23 x 33 cm) pans with parchment paper. If you only have one pan, that's okay. You'll just have to work in two batches. Place one batch of cookie dough in each pan. Using your hand and a spare piece of parchment paper, spread the dough out into an even layer in each pan. Place the pans into the freezer and allow the dough to freeze for at least 1 hour.

2. While the dough freezes, take the ice cream out of the freezer and allow it to soften. You don't want it to be completely melted, just soft enough to be easily spread.

3. When the dough and ice cream are ready, spread the ice cream evenly over one rectangle of dough. Carefully take the other dough rectangle out of its pan and place it face down onto the ice cream, peeling off the parchment paper. Placing it face down will give you a smooth surface for the outside of your sandwich. Place the giant sandwich back into the freezer for at least 1 hour to set.

4. When you want to serve the sandwiches, cut into 12 squares and serve immediately. You can store the sandwiches in their pan covered with plastic wrap or individually wrapped in plastic wrap for up to 1 month in the freezer.

Note:

If you want an extra-fun sandwich, instead of cutting them into squares, use cookie cutters to cut them into different shapes. You could use a simple circle cutter or holiday-themed cutters, like a Christmas tree or a heart for Valentine's Day.

COOKIE DOUGH LOG CAKE

YIELD: MAKES ONE 9 X 13-INCH (23 X 33 CM) CAKE

Now, just to get it out of the way from the get-go, there isn't actually any cake in this log cake. I've replaced the cake with cookie dough. I feel like everyone will be okay with that, though. Right? This recipe was actually one of the most fun recipes I got to create. It has a rich, fudgy ganache layer and a creamy, fluffy vanilla frosting layer. Maybe the best part of the cake is that I rolled it in rainbow sprinkles. I don't know about you, but in my opinion, everything is better with sprinkles. And it made it look beautiful! You can use any dough for this recipe.

1. Line a 9 x 13-inch (23 x 33 cm) pan with parchment paper, with the ends overlapping the sides of the pan.

2. Spread the cookie dough evenly in the pan. It will be a thin layer, so it may take a little finessing to get it into all four corners. I used my hands and a spare sheet of parchment paper, which I found was much easier than a spatula, but use whatever is works for you. Once done, place it in the freezer for at least 30 minutes or until the dough has hardened.

3. In a medium microwave-safe bowl, place the chocolate chips and heavy cream. Heat for 30 seconds on high and then stir until a smooth ganache forms. If not all of the chocolate chips melted, heat in 15-second intervals until completely melted.

4. Take the pan out of the freezer, scoop the ganache onto the dough, and spread it out evenly. I used an offset spatula, and it worked great. Once done, place it back into the freezer for another 30 minutes or until the ganache has set and hardened.

5. In the bowl of a stand mixer fitted with the whisk attachment or in a large bowl with a handheld mixer, whip the butter until it becomes very pale.

1 batch of edible cookie dough of choice

1½ cups (263 g) semisweet chocolate chips

¼ cup (60 ml) heavy cream

½ cup (112 g) unsalted butter, softened

1½ cups (180 g) confectioners' sugar

¾ teaspoon vanilla extract

Pinch of salt

2 to 3 tablespoons (28 to 45 ml) chocolate syrup

Rainbow sprinkles, for rolling the cake

CONTINUED ON NEXT PAGE

6. Add the confectioners' sugar a little at a time and mix on low until it's fully incorporated. Once the sugar is fully incorporated, begin to whip the frosting. It will grow in volume and become very light in color and texture. Whip for about 1 minute on high.

7. Add the vanilla and salt and whip until combined.

8. Take the pan out of the freezer and spread the frosting evenly over the ganache layer. Now that all of the layers are made, allow the pan to sit at room temperature so it can begin to thaw. The dough will need to be warmer so that it's pliable enough to roll into a log. Depending on the dough you used and how cold your freezer it, the thawing time may vary. It took mine about 45 minutes. You want it to still be somewhat cold, or else it will be too soft to roll cleanly. You'll know the dough is ready to roll when it will begin to roll on its own when you pick up one end of the parchment paper.

9. Lift one end of the parchment paper up and out of the pan slightly. Pull it toward the other end of the pan. The dough should begin to roll over on itself. Gently continue pulling the parchment paper over the beginning of the log and toward the other end of the pan. Use the parchment paper to your advantage. It really makes it much easier to roll the log instead of trying to do it with just your hands. Smooth out and shape the log as you go, again using the parchment paper.

10. When you have completed your roll and you have a log , place it back into the freezer and allow it to harden, at least another 30 minutes.

11. Meanwhile, get another pan (make sure it has sides and is big enough to fit the log) and cover the bottom in an even layer of rainbow sprinkles.

Note:
You don't have to use chocolate syrup to coat your cake. If your dough doesn't go with a chocolate flavor or you just prefer something other than chocolate, use another ice cream syrup, such as caramel, butterscotch, or white chocolate.

12. When the log has hardened, remove it from the freezer and get ready to paint it in chocolate syrup. And yes, I really do mean paint! Using a large pastry brush, paint the chocolate syrup over the outside of the log. It doesn't need to be a thick layer. In fact, it really should just be a thin layer. The point of the sauce isn't for its flavor, but rather to use it as "glue" for the sprinkles to stick to.

13. After you've painted the log with the sauce, take it by the ends and place it into the sprinkles. Carefully roll the log in the sprinkles. Use your hands to add more sprinkles to empty spaces and then pat them down so that you get full coverage.

14. The log is easiest to cut when it's cold. If it's too warm, cutting it will just squish the log down. It's best eaten closer to room temperature. Eat it immediately or cover tightly and store for up to 1 month in the refrigerator or 3 months in the freezer.

COOKIE DOUGH–FILLED GRAHAM CRACKERS

YIELD: MAKES 12 SANDWICHES

These cookie dough–filled graham crackers are a crunchy goodie that make a satisfying snack to eat after school or work. The graham cracker sandwiches are half-dipped in chocolate and sprinkled with toppings for a gourmet look. Use different types of chocolate and toppings to diversify the sandwiches. You could even dip one half in white chocolate, allow it to set, and then dip the other half in milk chocolate. Get creative with them. The possibilities are endless!

12 full-size graham crackers

1 batch of edible cookie dough of choice

2 cups (350 g) chocolate chips of choice

2 tablespoons (28 ml) vegetable oil

½ cup (weight will vary) topping of choice, for coating the sandwiches

1. Line a baking sheet with parchment paper. Carefully break each graham cracker in half.

2. Place about 3 tablespoons (45 g) of cookie dough onto a graham cracker square. Spread the dough out to the corners as best as you can with a butter knife or small spatula. Then, place another square on top of the dough. Squeeze it slightly so that the dough comes to the edges of the square. Run your knife over the edges of the squares to fix any dough that may have squeezed out too far.

3. Repeat for the remaining graham crackers and then place them onto the baking sheet. Place the baking sheet in the freezer for at least 30 minutes to allow the dough to firm up.

4. In a microwave-safe bowl, place the chocolate chips. Place the bowl in the microwave and heat on high in 20-second intervals. After each interval, stir the chips. Don't worry if the chips aren't melted after the first one or two intervals. We are faux-tempering the chocolate.

5. Once the chocolate is fully melted, add the oil. Mix it into the chocolate to create a thinner coating.

6. Take the graham cracker sandwiches out of the freezer and set up a little assembly line to dip and coat them with your toppings.

7. Dip half of a sandwich into the chocolate. Allow the excess chocolate to drip off back into the bowl before putting the sandwich back down on the baking sheet. Sprinkle the topping onto the top of the chocolate-dipped side of the sandwich.

8. Repeat for the remaining sandwiches and then place them back into the freezer so that the chocolate can set, about 5 minutes.

9. Eat immediately or store wrapped in plastic wrap for 1 week at room temperature, 1 month in the refrigerator, or 3 months in the freezer.

COOKIE DOUGH SUNDAE

YIELD: SERVES 3 OR 4

This isn't so much a recipe as it is a list of awesome ideas to help you make the perfect cookie dough sundae. I did include homemade butterscotch and whipped cream recipes that I totally recommend you topping your sundae off with. Be creative with this dessert. Use different kinds of ice cream and different kinds of cookie dough. Use a bunch of different toppings and sauces. Add a banana to make it a banana split. Add a warm brownie to make a brownie sundae. The possibilities are truly endless. Most important, don't forget the cherry on top!

1. In a large bowl, arrange the ice cream scoops.

2. Add one scoop of cookie dough on top of each scoop of ice cream.

3. Add the sauces and toppings and then dollop whipped cream on top of each cookie dough scoop.

4. Top each whipped cream mound with a cherry. Pass out the spoons and enjoy immediately!

3 scoops of ice cream of choice

3 scoops of (about ½ cup each) edible cookie dough of choice

Sauces of choice

Toppings of choice

Whipped cream

3 maraschino cherries

Note:
This sundae is meant to be served family style, but if you'd rather make individual servings, use one scoop of ice cream and one scoop of cookie dough per serving and top however you want!

Homemade Butterscotch

¼ cup (55 g) unsalted butter

½ cup (115 g) lightly packed brown sugar

⅓ cup (80 ml) heavy cream

1 teaspoon vanilla extract

1. In a medium saucepan, melt the butter over medium-high heat. When the butter has melted, mix in the brown sugar and heavy cream.

2. Bring to a boil and allow the mixture to boil for 2 to 3 minutes.

3. Remove from the heat and stir in the vanilla.

4. This is best eaten warm on your ice cream, as it becomes a thicker sauce as it cools. Just reheat it to regain the pourable consistency.

Homemade Whipped Cream

¾ cup (175 ml) heavy cream, cold

½ teaspoon vanilla extract

1 tablespoon (8 g) confectioners' sugar

1. In a large bowl, whip the heavy cream with a whisk or handheld mixer until it begins to thicken.

2. Add the vanilla and sugar and continue whipping until soft peaks form. If you prefer thicker whipped cream, keep whipping until you reach the consistency you want. But be careful not to overmix or else you will make butter!

Note:

If you choose to make the whipped cream, chill your bowl and beaters beforehand. This will help the cream whip up faster.

Acknowledgments

This book was an absolutely thrilling experience to write, and I couldn't have done it without many special people in my life. Thank you to all who helped me create this amazing book.

I'd first like to thank my boyfriend, Alex. You have supported Unbaked and me since Day 1. I truly couldn't have gotten here without you. Thank you for every cookie dough–covered dish you washed for me while I tested all of these recipes. Thank you for telling me this book was going to come out amazing when my depression would tell me it wasn't. Thank you for taking all of my packages to the post office. Thank you for cooking me dinners when I was too tired. Thank you for loving me. I am immensely blessed to wake up to you every day.

I'd like to thank my mom and dad, who have always supported my unconventional ways of achieving my dreams. Thank you, Mom, for dropping everything and driving two hours to help me with Unbaked and this book anytime I needed you. Thank you, Dad, for being my biggest cheerleader and helping me when I had no money to pay rent in the early days of Unbaked. Thank you both for being proud of me. Unbaked wouldn't be what it is today without you, and this book wouldn't have happened without your continued support.

I'd like to thank my little sister, Natalie, for helping me create this book. Thank you for being my taste tester when I was in a sugar coma from tasting so many cookie doughs in a day. Thank you for helping me come up with fun flavor combinations and for always being one of Unbaked's biggest fans.

I'd like to thank Erin Weise, the Cavataio family, Aunt Heather, and my cousin Jordan for helping me taste-test recipes, too.

I'd like to thank Tod Leonard for making me the writer I am today. Without you, I wouldn't be where I am today. Thank you for taking me under your wing and helping me not only in my career but in my life. I owe you so much and love being your friend and "daughter."

I'd like to thank Grammy for helping to teach me how to bake and reading everything I've ever written and saying it was great, even when it probably wasn't. Thank you to Grampy for keeping my spirits up with your fantastic stories.

Finally, I'd like to especially thank the Harvard Common Press, The Quarto Group, and Dan Rosenberg for giving me this incredible opportunity to write this book. You have allowed one of my biggest dreams to come true, and I will forever be grateful for you trusting in me to create this book. Thank you, Dan, for answering all of my millions of questions, no matter the time, and for walking me through writing my first book.

About the author

Olivia Hops is the founder and owner of Unbaked: A Cookie Dough Bar, an online shop specializing in customizable edible cookie dough. Before un-baking, the San Diego native was an avid sports fan, playing football throughout middle school and high school (and yes, with the boys!). She aspired to be a sports journalist and began her writing career at just 11 years old when she started writing for *Sports Illustrated Kids*. At 18, she moved from San Diego to Los Angeles to start what she thought was her dream job at the NFL Network. She quickly realized she wasn't cut out for sitting behind a desk and in 2015, the 19-year-old launched Unbaked. It became the world's first edible cookie dough shop that allowed its customers to customize their dough.

Index